# Heart of The Lions

## History of the Vernon High School Football Team

By Charles A. Owen & JT Smith

Cover by Sam Bursh, Special Artwork by Tony McDonald

**ISBN**
**Paperbound**     **9781735631042**
**Hardcover**     **9781735631059**

# Table of Contents

History.................................................................................................3

Snapshot of the School.....................................................................4

Football History .................................................................................5

1955-57 .............................................................................................5

1958-59 .............................................................................................5

1960 ..................................................................................................6

1961 ..................................................................................................8

1962 ................................................................................................10

1963 ................................................................................................14

1964 ................................................................................................22

1965 ................................................................................................29

1966 ................................................................................................34

1967 ................................................................................................39

1968 ................................................................................................51

1969 ................................................................................................53

End of the Era ................................................................................61

Special Addendum .........................................................................62

Special Thanks ...............................................................................91

Index ..............................................................................................92

# History of the Vernon High School

# Lions Football Team 1955-69

# By Charles A. Owen

This book is published to tell the story of the Vernon High School (VHS) Lions football team. A full and best-effort was made to compile this document. The time to fully tell the story of the team has sadly passed, because many of the principal contributors, players and supporters of the program have departed the confines of this earth. Many were gone before pen was put to paper. I believe all archived information that could be discovered is here and will be reported in these pages.

One of the reasons for creating this story is because it has never been done. As I discovered when writing Wampus Cat Football History, there is no one "in charge" of the history of things like public school football teams. If someone undertook the task of documenting and telling the story of the VHS Lions team, I have not found it, nor been told of it. So, as with the Wampus Cats, I've mostly relied on newspapers and firsthand accounts.

The main reason for writing this is because it *should* be done. For a little over a decade, the VHS Lions played football. They won the only State football championships in the history of Vernon Parish football, and they did it three times. They did it under difficult circumstances, to say the least; they had no home stadium, they were inadequately equipped and marginally supported by Parish school leadership, and they struggled to find opponents. The Lions accomplished much, however, and they generated a sense of pride and mystique that needs to be revisited and documented.

This review of results needs to be so much more. In future editions, I hope I can gain access to any additional former players and the remaining, living coaches and faculty from VHS. This edition contains a number of media reports and firsthand accounts from players and fans.

This book is dedicated to the students, alumni, faculty, staff, coaches and friends of the Mighty Vernon High School Lions.

# Snapshot of the School

Vernon High School was an educational institution in Leesville's Vernon Parish form 1937 – 1969.   From 1937 – 1958, the school was called was called the Vernon Parish Training Institute (VPTI).

Prior to 1937, there is no documented evidence of a formal school for African Americans in Vernon Parish.   The VPTI was built on Gladys Street in Leesville and the first principal was identified as a Professor Booke. The Rev. C.H. Washington was the second principal and served until 1942.  Professor Roy A. Rushen became principal in 1943.

The school was enlarged to 12 grades and was given the status as a high school in about 1943.   In 1953 Rushen helped secure funding to purchase a 10-acre tract of land to construct a new building on Nona Street. In November of 1953, students moved to the new VHS.   In 1958, VPTI was renamed Vernon High School.   Roy Rushen retired in 1966 and Fletcher Cheatham became principal and remained in that post until VHS was merged with Leesville High School in November of 1969.   Mr. Cheatham would return to the VHS location in 1981 as Principal of the newly formed Vernon Middle School, an integrated school.

Roy Rushen                    Fletcher Cheatham

# Football History

The Lions played football from 1955 – 1969.  Vernon played their athletic contests in an umbrella organization known as the Louisiana Interscholastic Athletic and Literary Association (LIALO).  The team had two head coaches, James Perkins from 1955-57 and Foster Thomas, from 1958-1969.   In the ensuing pages, the year-by-year record of the Lions will be reviewed.  Lists of coaches, players and accomplishments are found in these pages.   This project has been on-going for some time, and the author believes he has discovered all that is discoverable in the public domain.   To anyone reading this who knows of errors, omissions, or holes, please get in touch with the author so these things can be corrected.

## 1955-57

No records were discovered for Vernon games in the first three seasons of the program.  Joseph Martin, Vernon High School class of 1956, was a player on the first squad of VHS.    Mr. Martin relayed in a personal interview of the complexities of playing football in this time-period.  He spoke of challenges finding opponents and of deficiencies in equipment and facilities.  Mr. Martin recalled playing five or six games per year in the first few years.

## 1958 – 59

Foster Thomas was hired as the head coach of the Lions in 1958.  Joseph Deamer became an assistant for Coach Thomas.   Very little documented information was found in the research for this book on the early years.  A single news report from a 1958 game was discovered in the digital archives of the Leesville Leader. In this game, Vernon is reported as beating a team from Texas, Wiergate High.    Wiergate would appear a number of times on the Lions' schedules through the years and would be a reflection of the complexities of finding opponents and scheduling games for African American schools in Louisiana.   In the 1958 article, Thomas and Joseph Deamer were listed as coaches for the team.    Athletes named Miller, Haynes, Cheatham and Jefferson were listed as key players for the Lions in this article.  No other results could be found for the Lions in 1958 and 1959.

An interesting talk was given by Bro. White.

We adjourned to meet Oct. 9 at 7:30.

Mrs. Cecil Jeane, Sec.

## Vernon High Tops Weir Gate Gridders

The Vernon High School football team won their first game of the season last Saturday when they swamped the Weir Gate High School 38-6. The game was played at Weirgate.

Coaches Foster Thomas and Joseph Deamer claim they have the best prospects since football was started at Vernon Hi.

A. Roy Rushen, school principal, said, were are going good but we need to schedule more games.

We have some prospects that we hope will give us a full schedule.

Stars for Vernon Hi in last Saturday's game, were, Stors; Miller; Haynes; Cheatam and Jefferson.

**1960**

Reporting from the 1960 season was also nearly non-existent. No results were found in the digitized Leesville Leader for the year but reports from two games were listed in the Lake Charles American Press. The Lions lost both of the games, and both were shutouts. For posterity, the two articles are provided. No Vernon players, nor coaches are referenced in these articles, only the scores. No article was discovered for a game against Grand Avenue (Dequincy), and it occurred early in the season.

# Grand Avenue Turns Back Vernon, 8-0

LEESVILLE, La. (Spl.)—Grand Avenue of DeQuincy scored the only touchdown of the game in the third quarter, and staged strong defensive stands in its own territory to win an 8-0 football victory over Vernon high of Leesville.

The victory, third in a row for Grand Avenue, left the Tigers one victory away from the District 1-A championship. The crown will be decided when Grand Avenue tangles with Mossville October 28.

The Grand Avenue touchdown came on a 30-yard pass from Seymour Pullam to Leonard Brown, ending a 70-yard march. Pullam bucked over for the two-point conversion.

The Tigers were inside Leesville's 20 on two other occasions, but couldn't score. The Tigers themselves dug in twice to stop Leesville drives inside the Grand Avenue five. Prominent in the defensive line for Grand Avenue were guard Tom Rigmaiden and center Frank Williams, while half-an offensive standout.

| | | | | |
|---|---|---|---|---|
| Grand Avenue | 0 | 0 | 8 | 0— 8 |
| Vernon | 0 | 0 | 0 | 0— 0 |

GA—Leonard Brown 30 pass from Seymour Pullam (Pullam run).

## STATISTICS

| | GA | Vernon |
|---|---|---|
| First downs | 9 | 7 |
| Rushing yardage | 224 | 153 |
| Passing yardage | 132 | 145 |
| Passes | 4-11 | 6-17 |
| Passes intercepted by | 0 | 0 |
| Punts | 4-30 | 2-23 |
| Fumbles lost | 0 | 3 |
| Yards penalized | 50 | 45 |

# Mossville Blanks Vernon, 28-0

WEST LAKE (Spl.) — Ask any Mossville fan to name the outstanding athletes of their school and they'll answer Kelly, Kelly, Goodwin and Goodwin.

The athletes they'll be referring to, of course, are George and Joseph Kelly and Willard and Lionel Goodwin. The four youths compose a pair of brother acts which has accounted for Mossville's consistent ranking among the best in District 1-A competition.

Yesterday the Kellys and the Goodwins were up to their old tricks again as they powered the Pirates to a 28-0 shutout over the Vernon high Lions of Leesville here at Ram stadium. Played before a homecoming crowd, the victory kept the Pirates undefeated in district competition this year and gave Coach LaSalle Williams his first district crown after only one season as head coach at Mossville.

Each of the Kellys and each of the Goodwins personally scored touchdowns against the Lions Saturday and Lionel successfully converted twice for four additional points.

George Kelly, a 170-pound halfback, drew first blood early in the opening stanza on an off-tackle to his right after taking a pitchout from quarterback Thomas Porter. The play carried 86 yards and gave the Pirates a 6-0 lead after only four minutes of play.

Brother Joseph Kelly got into the act about midway in the first frame when he took the snap from Porter, headed to his right side-line and raced 90 yards to the end zone. Lionel Goodwin then made his first two-point conversion of the evening and the Pirates ended the quarter with a 14-0 lead.

Desperately trying to stem the tide, the Lions battled the Pirates to a 0-0 deadlock during the second and third quarters before the Mossville offensive machine began clicking again. This time it was the Goodwins' chance for glory.

On third down and 15 yards to go for a first, Porter handed off to Lionel Goodwin who powered his 175 pound straight up the middle of the Vernon line on a 25-yard sprint to the end zone. The tally came early in the fourth quarter and the two teams settled down to play scoreless ball until the waning minutes of the game.

With less than three minutes left to play, Porter, who attempted only three passes in the entire game, faded back, cocked his arm and connected with Willard Goodwin on a 40-yard pass play for the final touchdown of the contest. Lionel Goodwin again carried for the two-point conversion, putting Mossville out front 28-0.

With the District 1-A championship now secure, the Pirates will have to win at least two more playoffs before they try for the state crown. They will meet the Plaisance eleven either here or in Plaisance on November 19 for the zone title. Should they win that game, they will then meet the winners of the Northern region at a date to be specified by the Louisiana Interscholastic Athletic and Literary Association.

| | | | | |
|---|---|---|---|---|
| Vernon | 0 | 0 | 0 | 0— 0 |
| Mossville | 14 | 0 | 0 | 14—28 |

Mossville Scoring: TD—George Kelly (86 run), Joseph Kelly (90 run), Lionel Goodwin (25 run), Willard Goodwin (40 pass from Thomas Porter). PAT—Lionel Goodwin 2 (runs).

## STATISTICS

| | Vernon | Mossville |
|---|---|---|
| First downs | 8 | 12 |
| Rushing yardage | 85 | 451 |
| Passing yardage | 46 | 80 |
| Passes | 5-9 | 2-3 |
| Passes intercepted by | 0 | 1 |
| Punts | 4-29 | 1-30 |
| Fumbles lost | 1 | 1 |
| Yards penalized | 35 | 26 |

Results from three games were discovered for the 1961 season.  The Lions defeated DeRidder's Carver, Dequincy's Grand Avenue and lost to the Mossville Pirates.   In the Carver contest, stars of the game were listed as Steve Kennedy, Jack Garrett, and Louis Jefferson.   Of note in the contest with Carver is that research uncovered no instance of the Lions ever losing to the team from DeRidder.   In the Mossville game, Kennedy scored Vernon's lone touchdown in a 34-6 loss.   In a roundtable interview, a player from the 1961 team reported the squad went 5-6 on the season.

## Thursday, September 28, 1961

# Vernon High Lions Rip Way Past DeRidder Gridders

The Vernon High Lions, with its potent ground game, crushed the Carver High Eagles of DeRidder 28 to 7.

The first touchdown was scored early in the first quarter as quarterback Jack Garrett sneaked over from the three yard line, after fullback Robert Dickerson had galloped 47 yards from scrimmage to set up the tally

In the second quarter halfback Steve Kennedy scampered twenty yards for the second TD. This drive was also spearheaded by Dickerson.

The Eagles scored late in the second period. The half-time score was 14-7.

In the third quarter Garrett passed to tailback Louis Jefferson on a 45 yard touchdown play.

In the fourth quarter Kennedy replaced Garrett as quarterback and on the first play from scrimmage he pitched out to Jefferson who skirted right end for the fourth and final score.

The Lions young defensive team performed gallantly, holding Carver to only 15 yards rushing and 50 yards passing. The offensive line carried out their assignments superbly.

Tonight the Lions play Weirgate high school (col.) at Weirgate.

———(o)———

# Mossville Is 34-6 Victor Over Vernon

LEESVILLE, La. (Spl.) — The Mossville Pirates notched their first conference victory in District 1-A here Friday night with a 34-6 victory over the Vernon Lions.

Leeman Shankle got things underway for Mossville when he scored on a 53-yard pass play from Willard Goodwin in the first period. Shankle also scored in the third frame on a five-yard run.

Lionel Goodwin crossed over from four yards out in the second period to add another score. Vernon got its lone tally in the same period when Steve Kennedy scored on a 25-yard run.

A. K. Washington ran 62 yards in the third period to add to Mossville's score. Mossville's final touchdown came in the final period when Charles Harris hauled in a pass from Goodwin on a play covering 60 yards.

| | | | | |
|---|---|---|---|---|
| Mossville | 7 | 6 | 14 | 7—34 |
| Vernon | 0 | 6 | 0 | 0—6 |

MOSSVILLE SCORING: TD—Leeman Shankle 2 (53 pass from Willard Goodwin, 5 run), Lionel Goodwin (4 run), A. K. Washington (62 run), Charles Harris (60 pass from Goodwin). PAT—Washington (pass from Goodwin, run), Shankle 2 (5 run).

VERNON SCORING: TD—Steve Kennedy (25 run).

### STATISTICS

| | Mossville | Vernon |
|---|---|---|
| First downs | 9 | 4 |
| Rushing yardage | 235 | 197 |
| Passing yardage | 147 | 0 |
| Passes attempted | 11 | 7 |
| Passes completed | 6 | 0 |
| Passes intercepted by | 0 | 0 |
| Punts | 1 30 | 4 25 |
| Fumbles lost | 1 | 2 |
| Yards penalized | 65 | 5 |

9

# 1962:  The Winning Begins

The 1962 season would usher in genuine and documented winning at Vernon High School.   By the time the season ended, the Lions would notch sevens wins and suffer only two losses.   The season saw the Lions continue their annual rivalry with neighboring Carver High School from DeRidder and also with Weirgate from Texas.  The Lions suffered two losses on the season, one to Mossville and one to Grand Avenue.  Both games were one score affairs, and the team from Leesville could have easily gone undefeated on the season with a break or two.

1962 witnessed the emergence of an extraordinary player, Carl Howard.   Howard played extensively for four years at Vernon and probably set rushing records that could not be touched, had they been documented or archived.   In the early 1960s, the media rarely reported total rushing yards, but had a penchant for reporting touchdowns and points scored. Howard would be a prolific scorer his entire time in high school.  What is most amazing about Howard is that he was born with one arm.

Media reporting was limited in 1962, but research and extrapolation were used to ascertain final results.   In the 1964 season, media reporting indicates that Vernon would ascend to a 21-game winning streak that covered the end of the 1962 season, the 63 season and the 64 season.

Carl Howard

# Grand Avenue Takes 13-7 Win Over Vernon

### By CAL M. HARRISON

DEQUINCY (Spl.)—Coach Richard Brown's Grand Avenue Tigers took a 13-7 decision over the Vernon Lions of Leesville here at Tiger stadium Friday night to go ahead 1-0 in the contest for District 1-A honors.

The Vernon loss— their first of the season— eliminated the Lions from contension in the district.

Only one team now stands in the way of the Tigers' three-year quest for the district crown. That team is the Mossville Pirates, who dropped their third outing of the season 18-7 to Jonas Henderson high in New Iberia Friday.

The Vernon Lions had the Tigers beaten in the statistic column with 151 to 96 yards rushing and 38-40 yards passing. They also drew first blood in the contest early in the second stanza on a six-yard slant play by Carl Howard.

Vernon's marker culminated 76-yard drive during which the Lions picked up five first downs.

Aiding the cause was a 15-yard assessment against the Tigers.

Grand Avenue saw its first touchdown play ruled out by a penalty, but bounced back in the closing minutes of the second period to tie the contest 7-7 at the half.

The Tigers' first tally came on a breath-taking 33 - yard punt return by Freddie Gray. James Spiller converted via a run to even the score.

Scoring the deciding touchdown for the Tigers was Alvin Farris who hauled in a short pass from Gray and scampered 40 yards to paydirt.

The attempt at conversion failed, but the teams battled to a 0-0 deadlock in the final frame to give Grand Avenue its first conference victory of the season.

Vernon ............ 0 7 0 0—7
Grand Avenue ...... 0 7 6 0—13
VERNON SCORING: TD—Carl Howard (6 yd run) PAT—Robert Dicerson (run). GRAND AVENUE SCORING TD — Freddie Gray (33 yd) punt return); Alvin Farris (40 yd pass from Freddie Gray) PAT —James Spiller (run).

**STATISTIC S**

# All Three Local Negro Preps Will Play at Home on Friday

All three of Lake Charles' Negro prep football teams will be in action on their home fields Friday night but the top attraction will be staged at Washington stadium for a battle of unbeaten teams.

The Washington Indians, unbeaten, but once-tied, face Capitol of Baton Rouge, unbeaten in three games this season.

In other action, the W. O. Boston Panthers host Pemberton high of Marshall, Texas, at Wildcat stadium, while across the river, Mossville's Pirates, still trying for their first victory, take aim on Vernon of Leesville.

The other Calcasieu parish entry, Grand Avenue of DeQuincy, will be shooting for three straight victories when the Tigers host Peabody of Alexandria. Grand Avenue has whipped Carver and Wiergate, Texas, in previous outings.

Washington has rolled up 155 points while holding its foes to just one touchdown, with a soggy, 6-6 tie with Peabody the only blot on the record. The Indians attack is built around Buddis Guillory and Gerald Woodward, who have tallied 37 and 30 points, respectively.

Capitol, tagged as a big, strong defensive club by scouts, has rolled past Scotlandville and Opelousas in addition to a 14-6 victory over Boston.

Boston, seeking to avenge a 20-14 loss to Pemberton last season, will be hampered by the absence of passing ace Delma Bennett, sidelined with a fractured foot.

Still around to provide firepower are George Walker, the bi-parish scoring leader with 43 points, and Paul DeJean and William Redfud, each of whom has tallied four touchdowns.

Providing formidable opposition for the struggling Pirates is a Vernon club that has posted victories over Carver and Willgate, Texas, since an opening loss to Grand Avenue of DeQuincy.

Coach LaSalle Williams says his club will be at full strength.

**PROBABLE STARTERS**

| PEMBERTON | Pos. | W.O.BOSTON |
|---|---|---|
| Howard (170) | L E | Goyen (175) |
| Woolen (240) | L T | Belford (180) |
| Thomas (165) | L G | Mthws (190) |
| Mitchell (160) | C | Hartman (185) |
| Boyd (180) | R G | Poole (210) |
| Watson (224) | R T | Hebert (195) |
| Horn (170) | R E | Stevens (180) |
| Bousley (170) | Q B | DeJean (180) |
| Stouts (180) | L H | Redfud (162) |
| Gray (148) | R H | Walker (175) |
| Stevens (188) | F B | Vallery (168) |

THURS., OCT. 11, 1962, Lake Charles American Press

SAT., OCT. 13, 1962, Lake Charles American Press.

# Mossville Cops First Victory of Season 7-6

WEST LAKE (Spl.) — A victory, although a narrow one, was a pleasant one for Mossville here Friday night.

It was the Pirates' first one of the 1962 grid season.

Mossville scored first, got the all-important extra point, and then eased to a slim 7-6 triumph over visiting Vernon of Leesville.

The Pirates A. K. Washington set up and scored the Mossville tally. Washington scampered for 21 yards to the Vernon one, then the next time around plunged over. Leemon Shankle ran the extra point.

In the third period, Carl Howard got the lone Vernon score with a three yard jump at the goal line. The extra point try failed.

Mossville played a fine defensive game, holding Vernon to just 49 yards rushing and five first downs, while the Pirates compiled 160 yards on the ground and added up eight first downs.

The passing for both teams was ineffective. Vernon got the better of it with 34 yards on five of nine attempts. Mossville hit on one pass for no gain in four tries.

Leading the Pirate defense was right tackle Richard Lee who was credited with 13 individual tackles.

| | | | | |
|---|---|---|---|---|
| Vernon | 0 | 0 | 6 | 0—6 |
| Mossville | 0 | 7 | 0 | 0—7 |

VERNON SCORING: TD—Carl Howard (3 run).

MOSSVILLE SCORING: TD—A. K. Washington (1 run). PAT—Leemon Shankle (run).

**STATISTICS**

| | Vernon | Mossville |
|---|---|---|
| First downs | 5 | 8 |
| Rushing yardage | 49 | 160 |
| Passing yardage | 34 | 0 |
| Passes | 5-9 | 1-4 |
| Passes intercepted by | 0 | 1 |
| Punts | 2-25.0 | 1-15.0 |
| Fumbles lost | 1 | 4 |
| Yards penalized | 75 | 66 |

12

The James Stephens High School band (top photo) and Homecoming Queen's float (smaller photo) were the high points of the school's homecoming parade here Friday afternoon. The colorful band, which annually attracts hundreds to the parade, is under the direction of Jewel Douglas and is lead by drum major Leroy Mouton. Members of the court are Queen Annie Lee Vidrine, daughter of Mr. and Mrs. Olenes Vidrine, and maids Inez Lafleur, daughter of Mr. and Mrs. Gerald Lafleur, and Barbara Thomas, daughter of Mr. and Mrs. Linton Thomas. Other units participating in the parade were the Elementary queen's float, W. W. Stewart High School Band, Boy Scouts and other marching units. James Stephens lost the homecoming football game to Vernon High School of Leesville, 36-0. The Stephens team is coached by Curley Dossman.

NOTE: This is media article from a paper in South Louisiana. Vernon's win is mentioned in passing, but does provide documentation of the contest

# 1963: The First Championship

The Vernon Lions earned their first state title during the 1963 team.  Coach Thomas's team finished the regular season with a record of nine wins and zero losses and brought the first ever football championship of any type to Vernon Parish.

Vernon High School (VHS) was impressive on both sides of the ball in the 1963 campaign.  The season included two wins over Plaisance, a third consecutive win over Carver and big victories over schools from East Texas (Wiergate and Lincoln).   The closest game of the year was a five-point win over Paul Breaux of Lafayette Parish.  Neither of the post season games were close and the state championship game was a dominating 33-0 performance.

| Game date | W | L | | | | |
|---|---|---|---|---|---|---|
| 6-Sep | W | | Vernon | 48 | Plaisance | 2 |
| 13-Sep | W | | Vernon | 48 | Carver (DeRidder) | 0 |
| 6-Oct | W | | Vernon | 20 | Wiergate (Texas) | 0 |
| 13-Oct | W | | Vernon | 52 | Plaisance | 0 |
| 27-Oct | W | | Vernon | 19 | Paul Breaux | 14 |
| 1-Nov | W | | Vernon | 38 | Lincoln (Texas) | 16 |
| 8-Nov | W | | Vernon | 13 | Grand Avenue (DeQuincy) | 0 |
| 15-Nov | W | | Vernon | 19 | Wesley Ray | 0 |
| 23-Nov | W | | Vernon | 33 | Good Pine | 0 |
| | 9 | 0 | | | | |

Sophomore Carl Howard was the offensive star of the 1963 squad.  Box scores and articles for 1963 were more plentiful than most years, but cumulative rushing yards were not tracked nor disseminated in the media.   It's easy to imagine Howard rushing for over 1,000 yards on the season, but no documentation exists to validate this assumption.   He did score over 10 touchdowns for the season and was one of the unquestioned stars of the 63 squad. Other key contributors were Louis Jefferson, Robert Burns, Robert Dickerson, David Gaines, and JT Smith.  Louis Jefferson and Otis Williams signed to play at the collegiate level with Wiley College (Texas).

Game Notes

| | |
|---|---|
| Plaisance | Carl Howard and Louis Jefferson scored 3 x TDs |
| Carver (DeRidder) | Third straight victory over Carver; Carl Howard multiple TDs |
| Wiergate (Texas) | Robert Burns 2 x TDs |
| Plaisance | No articles or box scores discovered |
| Paul Breaux | Homecoming win, closest game of the season |
| Lincoln (Texas) | Howard rushed for 125, Robert Dickerson 95 yds rushing |
| Grand Avenue (DeQuincy) | Louis Jefferson rushed for 85, Howard rushed for 65 |
| Wesley Ray | Playoff Game; JT Smith TD pass to Dickerson |
| Good Pine | First State Championship; Carl Howard multiple TDs |

# Vernon Rips By Plaisance

LEESVILLE (Spl.) — The Vernon High school Lions rode the flying heels of Carl Howard and Louis Jefferson to a 48-2 triumph over Plaisance here Saturday night.

Howard and Jefferson e a c h scored three touchdowns and J. T. Smith added another as the Lions completely outclassed the visitors.

```
Plaisance ............... 0  0  0  2— 2
Vernon   ...............21 14  7  6—48
```

V—Carl Howard, 25 run. Robert Dickerson run.
V—Louis Jefferson, 45 intercepted pass. Robert Dickerson run.
V—Carl Howard, 15 run. Robert Dickerson run.
V—J. T. Smith, 2 run. Robert Dickerson run.
V—Louis Jefferson, 25 run. Robert Dickerson run.
V—Carl Howard, 10 run. Robert Dickerson run.
P—Safety, J. T. Smith tackled in end zone by Hule Fontenot.
V—Louis Jefferson, 15 run. Run failed.

# Vernon High Rips Carver 48-0 for 3rd Straight Year

The Vernon High Lions with a devastating ground and air attack crushed the Carver High Eagles of DeRidder, 48-0 at De-Ridder, Saturday night. The fans had hardly settled in their seats as Carl Howard on the second play from scrimmage took a hand-off from quarterback J. T. Smith and scampered twenty-five yards behind beautiful blocking for the first touchdown. The second T. D. came as half-back Louis Jefferson bulled his way off tackle for 15 yards. The rest of the scoring went like this, George Williams scored on a 25 yard pass from J. T. Smith. Robert Dickerson burst through the middle of the line for 10 yards and scored. Halfback Herbert Burnes scored two T. D.'s on beautiful runs of 25 and 15 yards.

Vernon scored a safety for 2 points as line-backer Steve Williams tackled Carver's quarterback in his own end zone. The Eagles complete offense was held at bay by the outstanding play of ends, Tyron Burkehead and Clinton Williams.

Line-backers Barney Wilson, Steve Williams, Robert Johnson and Andrew Johnson completely frustrated the Eagles air and ground game. We want to thank the many persons who traveled with us to DeRidder. This in itself was indeed a great moral factor in our winning.

# Vernon High Lions Roll Over Wiergate By 20-0 Margin

The Vernon High Lions getting off to a slow start in the first half scoring only six points in the first quarter as H. B. Herbert Burns raced 15 yrds to the end zone for the six pointer, the point after failed

The Lions came back in the second half as the Panthers kicked off to the Lions and again Herbert Burns took the kickoff on the 10 yrd line and raced 90 yrds in for his second touchdown The offensive line displayed excellent blocking spearheaded by Charles Smith, Frankie Williams, Joseph Clarkston, and Tommy Joe Robinson.

The Lions came back in the fourth quarter and Robert Dickerson raced in for another six pointer from 22 yrds. out, both of the points after touchdown were scored by Robert Dickerson, F.B. The Lions Defensive team again displayed superb defense by allowing the Panthers only 63 yrds rushing and 20 yrds. passing.

16

# Vernon High Lions Claw Way Past Paul Breax

Vernon High's Lions 1963 - 64 homecoming victory was a big success, although there probably were still many hearts fluttering Saturday morning after Friday night's game.

With less than three minutes left to play, Vernon's George Williams shook the ball loose from Paul Breaux's All-State full-back Major Lincoln with a crushing tackle to set up the winning touchdown.

At this stage of the game Paul Breaux led Vernon 14-13. The lions moved the ball 70 yards with the hard running and much used Carl Howard and Hebert Burns. Howard scored from three yards out after Louis Jefferson had switched from end to half-back to pick up ground on runs of 15 and 10 yards. This victory was a great team effort as both offensive and defensive units played their hearts out against a cocky and over-confident South Louisiana team. This was by far the toughest assignment for the Lions so far.

The Lions will try to spoil San Augustine, Texas' homecoming this Saturday, November 2.

On November 8, the Lions will host the Grand Avenue Tigers of DeQuincy for the all important district championship.

"We want to thank the many wonderful persons who turned out to see the game which climaxed a wonderful homecoming day," said A Roy Rushen, school principal. "We hope to have your continued support at our next game and at games in years to come "

---

be the same with beef if a white-face was treated as some hunters treat deer.

Five a day is the limit on geese, on which the season opens Thursday, Nov. 7. The limit can include two speckle-bellies, but no Canada geese.

## Vernon High Lions Wallop Texas Team by 38-16 Margin

The Vernon High Lions behind the running of Robert Dickerson and Carl Howard completely out-classed the Lincoln High Tigers of San Augustine, Texas Saturday night.

The Tigers scored first as quarterback Joe Brown connected with half-back Robert Jones on a jump pass over center. Then for the rest of the game the Tigers were wondering where to look for Dickerson and Howard.

Dickerson by far played his best game as he gained 95 yards on 12 carries. Howard gave a stellar performance as usual as he ground out 125 yards on 15 carries. Quarterback J. T. Smith kept the Tigers defense wondering as he mixed his plays beautifully.

Dickerson by far played his on runs of 8 and 20 yards, on both runs he was hit, but kept his momentum and hit pay dirt. Howard scored once on an end sweep of 40 yards as he picked his holes beautifully behind pulling guards Tommy Joe Robinson and Frankie Ray Williams. Hebert Burns scored once on a three yard burst and quarterback J. T. Smith sneaked over from the two yard stripe to end the scoring. The Lions defensive unit had its hands full trying to contain the big Tiger backs, as they continually ground out great yardage.

The Lions were preping for this weeks District Championship with the ever tough Grand Avenue Tigers of DeQuincy. The

Lions are in excellent mental and physical condition. It is believed that if the Lions are victorious Friday night here in Leesville, Vernon High may have it's first State Championship team.

## CARD OF THANKS

We want to thank our many friends for their beautiful floral offerings and sympathy after the death of our beloved mother. Our special thanks to Dr. Butler and Rev. Werner, and to all the members of the First Baptist Church of Leesville, for the food and many other kindnesses shown us at this trying time.

The family of
Mrs. Nancy Lea Ford

17

# Lions Are District Champions; Playoff Game Here Friday

The Vernon "Lions" reign as District 1-A Champions for the first time by virtue of a 13-0 triumph Friday night over the Grand Avenue Tigers.

The Lions struck for a first period score by marching 50 yards. Louis Jefferson got the last 10 for the six-pointer and Robert Dickerson ran over the extra point.

A recovered fumble set up the Lions' next score with Jefferson turning in a sparkling 35 yard scoring run. Jefferson had 85 yards in only four carries, while teammate Carl Howard had 65 in seven attempts.

Outstanding defensive play was turned in by tackle Frankie Williams, guard Tommy Joe Robinson and guard Charles Smith for Vernon.

Vernon High will host Wesley Ray High School of Angie, for Southern Division Champions on Nov. 16, at 7:30 p.m. here in Leesville.

| | | | | |
|---|---|---|---|---|
| Grand Avenue | 0 | 0 | 0 | 0— 0 |
| Vernon High | 7 | 0 | 0 | 6—13 |

V—Louis Jefferson, 10 run Robert Dickerson run.

V—Louis Jefferson, 35 run Run failed

| | GA | V |
|---|---|---|
| First Downs | 4 | 7 |
| Rushing Yardage | -34 | 103 |
| Passing Yardage | 0 | 0 |
| Passes | 0-12 | 1-2 |
| Passes Intercepted | 1 | 0 |
| Punts | 1 | 0 |
| Fumbles lost | 3 | 2 |
| Yards Penalized | 110 | 189 |

# Vernon Blanks Wesley Ray 19-0 In Playoff Tilt

LEESVILLE (Spl.)—The Vernon Parish Lions blanked Wesley Ray of Angie 19-0 here Saturday night to win the southern regional Negro class A football championship.

The Lions will play Goodpine of Jena next Saturday for the state championship.

```
Wesley  Ray ...............0  0  0  0—0
Vernon      ...............13 0  6  8—19
```

V—Carl Howard, 1 run. Kick failed.
V—Louis Jefferson, 20 run. Carl Howard run.
V—Charles Smith, 45 run with fumble. Kick failed.

## STATISTICS

|                        | Vernon | Wesley |
|------------------------|--------|--------|
| First Downs            | 7      | 2      |
| Rushing yardage        | 146    | 21     |
| Passing yardage        | 41     | 28     |
| Passes                 | 3-7    | 2-13   |
| Passes intercepted by  | 2      | 0      |
| Punts                  | 4-35   | 5-25   |
| Fumbles lost           | 2      | 2      |
| Yards penalized        | 20     | 40     |

# Vernon Hi Wins State Crown At Good Pine

The undefeated Vernon High Lions won the Louisiana Negro class "A" football championship Saturday night by routing the Good Pine Wildcats 33-0.

Carl Howard led the Lions with two touchdowns as they captured their ninth straight decision. Howard scored on runs of 56 and 25 yards.

Steve Williams scored one touchdowns on a 56-yard run with a pass interception and Robert Dickerson and Herbert Burns got the others on runs of three and nine yards, respectively.

| | | | | |
|---|---|---|---|---|
| Vernon ........7 | 0 | 19 | 7—33 |
| Good Pine.. 0 | 0 | 0 | 0— 0 |

V—Carl Howard, 56 run. Herbert Burns run.

V—Robert Dickerson, 3 run. Run failed.

V—Carl Howard, 25 run. Run failed.

V—Steve Williams, 56 intercepted pass. Louis Jefferson run

V—Herbert Burns, 9 run. Louis Jefferson rsun.

| | Vernon | Good Pine |
|---|---|---|
| First downs | 6 | 8 |
| Rushing yardage | 256 | 78 |
| Passing yardage | 82 | 54 |
| Passes | 2-6 | 3-16 |
| Passes int. | 1 | 0 |
| Punts | 240 | 4-15 |
| Fumbles lost | 2 | 0 |
| Yards penalized | 110 | 37 |

Lions record—1963

Lions 48; Lions 49; Lions 22; Lions 48, Plaisance 2; Lions 49, DeRidder 0; Lions 22; Wiergate, Texas 0; Lions 52, Plaisance 0; Lions 20, Paul Breaux 14; Lions 38, San Augustine, Texas 16; Lions 13, DeQuincy 0; Lions 19, Wesley Ray 0; Lions 33, Good Pine 0.

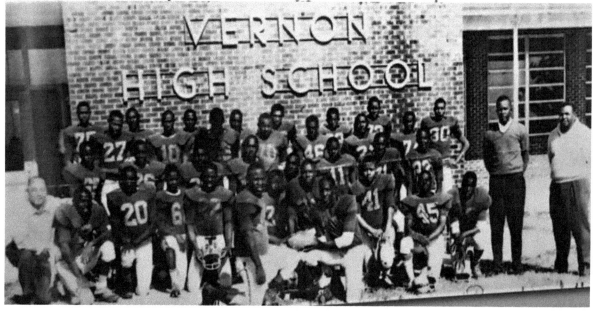

Principal Roy Rushen and Quarterback JT Smith with the State Championship Trophy

# 1964: Another Stellar Season

In sports dialect, the phrase "hangover" is often associated with teams who have claimed championships. Many times, teams who have had great seasons one year often falter in the ensuing year because of the jubilance and celebration of the previous year's title. No such thing occurred for the Vernon Lions in 1964. Coach Foster Thomas' team picked up where they left off in 63 and reeled off 7 consecutive wins.

The Lions took down teams from Opelousas, DeRidder, Dequincy, Many, Lafayette and Moss Bluff. This string of wins included five shut out wins, and the Lion defense only surrendered scores three times all season.

Sadly, one of the games the Lions allowed their endzone to be penetrated was in the final game of the year. In the first round of the LIALO playoffs, the Lions gave up a lone touchdown, but failed to score themselves, thus ending a perfect season to that point and ending an impressive 21 game winning streak that started in 1962. In a round-table interview with players, the story of how the Wesley Ray game ended was brought up and it was noted by more than one player that as Carl Howard was racing down the sidelines to score a tying touchdown late in the game, a player from the opposing team came off the sideline and tackled Howard, preventing the score. This call was apparently missed by the officiating crew and the Lions winning streak came to an unceremonious and controversial end.

| Game Date | W | L | | | | | |
|-----------|---|---|--------|----|------------------------|----|
| 5-Sep | W | | Vernon | 25 | Plaisance (Opelousas) | 0 |
| 12-Sep | W | | Vernon | 34 | Carver (DeRidder) | 6 |
| 18-Sep | W | | Vernon | 13 | Grand Avenue (Dequincy) ✦ | 0 |
| 3-Oct | W | | Vernon | 34 | Sabine (Many) | 0 |
| 9-Oct | W | | Vernon | 39 | Plaisance | 0 |
| 23-Oct | W | | Vernon | 14 | Paul Breaux (Lafayette) | 12 |
| 30-Oct | W | | Vernon | 6 | Mossville | 0 |
| 6-Nov | | L | Vernon | 0 | Wesley Ray (Angie) | 6 |
| | 7 | 1 | | | | |

The 1964 season witnessed the continued dominance of the Lion offense. Running back sensation Carl Howard continued to be hyper productive on the ground and at times as a receiver. Sophomore quarterback JT Smith was noted throwing a number of touchdown passes. Other offensive stars included Herbert Burns and David Gaines. Some defensive stars from the team were Frankie Williams, Clearance Kennedy, Glenn Garner and Steve Williams.

Game Notes

| Plaisance (Opelousas) | Carl Howard, 4 touchdowns; 3 running, 1 TD pass from JT Smith |
|---|---|
| Carver (DeRidder) | Howard 108 yards rushing, 3 TDs; JT Smith TD pass to Spencer |
| Grand Avenue (Dequincy) | Carl Howard 2 touchdowns |
| Sabine (Many) | Carl Howard 2 touchdowns; Clearance Kennedy pick 6 TD |
| Plaisance | Herbert Burns 165 yards rushing, 10 carries |
| Paul Breaux (Lafayette) | JT Smith TD pass to David Gaines; Carl Howard 1 rushing TD |
| Mossville | David Gaines TD pass from Roy Robinson |
| Wesley Ray (Angie) | 21 Game Winning Streak Ends |

L-R:   Clearance Kennedy, Glenn Garner, Carl Howard

# Lions Roar, Carver High Falls 34-6

The Vernon High Lions continued to roll as they completely outclassed the Carver Eagles of DeRidder 34-6 Friday night at Wampus Cats Stadium.

Vernon scored early in the first quarter as defensive tackle Frankie Williams broke through the Eagle line and nailed half-back James Williams in his own end zone for a safety and two points. Right halfback Hebert Burns enjoyed a fine night as he scored one of Vernon's five touchdowns on a four yard slant. Burns picked up 81 yards on 9 carries.

Vernon's spectacular one-armed half-back Carl Howard scored three touchdowns on runs of 4, 5, and 53 yards respectively. Howard gained 108 yards on 12 carries. Of nine touchdowns scored by Vernon in its first two games, Howard has 7 of them.

Quarterback J. T. Smith hit right end Alfred Spencer with a touchdown pass good for 26 yards. Vernon basically a ball-control team let all visiting coaches and scouts know that it too has air game. Smith completed 7 out of 8 passes for a total of 160 yards.

The Eagle offense was held in check as Vernon strong defensive unit anchored by 5' x 6" David Gaines allowed only a total of 60 yards gained. Eagle quarterbacks were completely frustrated as they attempted 6 passes without completion.

The Eagles only score came late in the game as reserve quarter back Roy Robinson fumbled a snap from center. The ball was scooped up and carried 65 yards by linebacker John Thomas for the score.

———(o)———

# Vernon Comeback Halts DeQuincy

The Vernon High Lions with their backs against the wall, came from behind to defeat Grand Avenue High 13 to 6 at DeQuincy Friday night.

The Lions won the toss and elected to receive. Vernon marched 50 yards to the Tigers 40 yard line before they were stopped by a determined Tiger line. Following exchange of punts the Tigers began to roll as halfback Robert Simms found a huge hole open on the left side of the line and scampered 75 yards for a 6 - 0 first quarter lead.

Vernon's great pair of middle guards, Frankie Williams and Charles Smith broke through and blocked the extra point attempt.

The Lions came back with scores in the second and fourth quarters to ice the victory. Carl Howard and Hebert Burns scored touchdowns for Vernon. Howard also added the extra point. Howard, Burns and Eddie Martin were the big guns for Vernon.

Linebackers, Steve Williams, Archie Pea and Ralph Lee recovered from an early mistake and did a fine job in holding the Tigers fast backs at bay.

The Lions had ample support as nearly 200 fans from Leesville made the trip. Vernon High would like to thank those persons for their continued support.

The Lions will host Sabine High of Many on October 3, for the next game at Wampus Cat Stadium. Game time 7:30 p.m.

———(o)———

24

# Vernon Lions Rip Sabine 34-0 For 18th Straight

The Vernon High Lions continued their winning ways as they completely outclassed Sabine High of Many, 34 - 0 Saturday night at Wampus Cat Stadium.

Vernon's last defeat was to Mossville early in 1962, since then the Lions have racked up 18 straight victories.

Hebert Burns, Carl Howard and quarterback J. T. Smith completely frustrated the waves of Many. Howard scored 13 points, Burns tallied 7, Smith 6, and defensive tackle Joe Clarkston picked up a fumble that linebacker Steve Williams shook loose from Many's Richard Garner with a vicious tackle and romped 15 yards for the final tally.

Defensive halfback Clarence Kennedy picked off a Many pass and scampered 65 yards for another tally. However this score was nullified by a clipping penalty.

Although the victory was a total team effort Vernon coaches were happy to see a fine job turned in by newcomers John Foster, Henry Jackson and Alvoy Wilson.

The Lion's next game will be Plaisance Indians in Leesville Saturday night, October 10.

## Vernon Rips Plaisance

The Vernon High Lions extended their winning streak to 19 straight games as they completely outplayed an outclassed Plaisance eleven of Opelousas Saturday night at Wampus Cat's Stadium 39-0.

The Lions built an early lead as first unit players scored three touchdowns and led 21 - 0 at the half. Carl Howard, Herbert Burns, and David Gains scored all of Vernon's points. Howard tallied 27 points, Burns 6, and Gains 6 on a beautiful pass from quarterback J. T. Smith.

Howard now leads in total scoring in Southwest Louisiana with 89 points, according to the Lake Charles American Press. His closest rival is C. Joiner of W. O. Boston of Lake Charles with 67 points.

Vernon's Herbert Burns was the leading ground gainers with 165 yards on 10 carries.

The Lions success thus far has been a total team effort. With the type of blocking furnished up front by Charles Smith, Sylvester Tinsley, and Robert Black the average back can excel.

Vernon's next two gamesg will prove if they rate to recognition they have received. The Lions will travel to Lafayette to play Paul Breaux a 3A power on Oct. 23. They return home to host powerful Mossville on · Oct. 31. Mossville was the last team to defeat Vernon 7-6 early in 1962. The Pirates boast a 5-0 record against strong opposition.

## Vernon Gets Number 20; Beats Paul Breaux By 14-12 Margin

The Vernon High Lions rolled up their 20th straight victory Friday night by edging past the Paul Breaux Tigers of Lafayette 14-12.

The mighty Lions had to overcome a 6-0 deficit in the first quarter to get the win. The host Tigers' Irving Walker had scored on a 10-yard run to put the Lions in a hole. Quarterback J. T. Smith and David Gaines teamed up on a pass play to score Vernon's first tally. Gaines made the TD on a 35-yarder from Smith. The conversion point put Vernon out front 7-6.

Vernon's touchdown machine, one-armed Carl Howard marked up a 4th quarter touchdown from 4 yards out to give the Lions their final six-pointer. The winning points were conversions by Howard and Herbert Burns.

Vernon won the statistics battle, too. The Lions, defending state Class A champs, ran for 187 yards and passed for 74 more on 7 good tosses in 12 tries. They made 9 first downs. PB picked up 185 rushing and 17 in the air. This was good for 5 firsts.

Mossville, the last team to beat the Lions comes to Leesville Oct. 31 to see if they can do it again. They stopped Vernon 7-6 way back in early 1962. Mossville is one of the powerhouse teams of the state this year and will be a severe test for Vernon's all-winning eleven.

———(o)———

## Thursday, November 5, 1964

# Vernon Lions Blanks Mossville Pirates 6-0 In Battle Of The Unbeaten

Vernon High School's Lions won the battle of the titans here Saturday night, beating the Mossville Pirates, 6-0.

It was Vernon's 21st straight victory and the seventh this season, and the first loss for Mossville after six triumphs in a row.

The Lions pushed over the winner in the third quarter after J. T. Smith intercepted a Pirate pass at the Vernon 24 and raced all the way to the Mossville 10 before he was overhauled.

Three plays moved the ball to the seven. On the fourth down, the Lions set up a field goal formation and then turned it into a touchdown pass with Roy Robinson pitching to David Gaines.

It was a battle of defense all the way.

Vernon penetrated to the Pirate 10 after a 55-yard march but lost the ball on downs in the first quarter. In the second, Vernon reached the eight but could not get the rest of the needed yardage.

Mossville drove to the Lion three in the third period but a penalty cost five and a fourth-down pass failed. In the fourth, the Pirates got to the ten but Vernon's Frankie Williams turned in a top defensive performance, counting 16 tackles and making two key pass interceptions.

| | | | | |
|---|---|---|---|---|
| Mossville | 0 | 0 | 0 | 0 - 0 |
| Vernon | 0 | 0 | 6 | 0 - 6 |

V-David Gaines 7-yard pass from Robinson. Run failed.

# Vernon Aims For Playoff Win Friday

A bidistrict playoff game between Vernon of Leesville at Angie Friday heads a light week of Southwest Louisiana Negro football action.

Only other game on tap is a Saturday contest between Mossville and Carver at DeRidder.

Vernon pits its 7-0 record on the line Friday against Angie. Carl Howard, the leading scorer in Southwest Louisiana, will be the main offensive threat for coach Foster Thomas.

Howard has tallied 15 touchdowns and six extra points in seven games for a whopping 96 points. Vernon overcame its biggest obstacle of the season so far by stopping Mossville, 6-0, in a district thriller last week.

The Pirates (6-1) try to bounce back against Carver Saturday. Carver has not won a ball game this year and will have its hands full trying to stop the dashing runs of Leemon Shankle and Edward McKeever.

Shankle is the third leading scorer in Southwest Louisiana with eight touchdowns and 16 extra points. McKeever has tallied 45 markers for a hold on seventh place.

## Wesley Ray Squeezes By Vernon High

Football is a game played in four quarters. Wesley Ray of Angie played good football four quarters. Vernon High played good football three quarters. The score Wesley Ray 6—Vernon 0.

The Vernon High Lions after winning 21 straight games fell victims to a spirited and vastly improved Wesley Ray eleven of Angie, located two miles from the Mississippi state line.

The Lions won the toss and elected to receive. A couple of running plays and a pass failed to net a first down. The Lions punted and in the next series of plays the game was settled. As the Eagles kept control of the ball and scored with the game only four minutes old.

The Lions fought back gamely time and time again only to have costly penalties stepped off against them when it appeared they had something going.

Quarterback J. T. Smith fumbled a second down snap and the Eagles recovered the fumble and ran the clock out. The victory earned the Eagles a play-off berth against Trout-Goodpine of Jena, the North Louisiana represenative, for the Class A Championship.

The Lions, however, enjoyed a successful season as they wound up with a 7-1 record including a 6-0 victory over powerful Mossville.

### Statistics

|                        | Ver. | W.R. |
|------------------------|------|------|
| First Downs            | 13   | 14   |
| Rushing Yardage        | 190  | 241  |
| Passing Yardage        | 53   | 0    |
| Passes                 | 0-8  | 5-11 |
| Passes intercepted by  | 1    | 2    |
| Punts                  | 1-30 | 3-32 |
| Fumbles lost           | 1    | 0    |
| Yards Penalized        | 55   | 20   |

### VERNON
(7-1)

Coach:
Foster Thomas

| 25 Plaisance   | 0  |
|----------------|----|
| 34 Carver      | 61 |
| 13 Gr. Avenue  | 6  |
| 34 Sabine      | 0  |
| 39 Plaisance   | 0  |
| 14 Paul Breaux | 12 |
| 6 Mossville    | 0  |
| 165 Total      | 24 |

(Zone)

| 0 Angie       | 6  |
| 165 Gr. Total | 30 |

27

CARL HOWARD • Right Halfback
Leading Scorer in State with 119 Points;
All-State Halfback; Eleventh Grade.

J. T. SMITH • Quarterback
All-State Quarterback

FRANKIE RAY WILLIAMS • Right Guard
All-State Guard; Captain of Team.

Head Coach Foster Thomas

Coach Samuel Bursh

Coach Fletcher Cheatham

Coach Joseph Deamer

28

# 1965

In the decade's middle season, the Lions again achieved a winning record. Playoffs were not in the cards for VHS in this year. Finding teams to play was difficult for all African-American schools, and the Lions were no exception. The Lions finished the season 5-2, but did not advance into the LIALO playoffs.

| Game Date | W | L | | | | | |
|-----------|---|---|------|-----|-------------------------|-----|
| 10-Sep | W | | Vernon | 13 | Carver (DeRidder) | 0 |
| 17-Sep | W | | Vernon | 33 | St Matthew | 7 |
| 24-Sep | | L | Vernon | 14 | Grand Avenue (Dequincy) | 18 |
| 8-Oct | W | | Vernon | 13 | Plaisance | 7 |
| 25-Oct | W | | Vernon | 12 | Carver (Bunkie) | 6 |
| 30-Oct | | L | Vernon | 13 | Mossville | 14 |
| 6-Nov | W | | Vernon | 28 | Wiergate | 12 |

JT Smith and Carl Howard continued to be major stars for the Lions in the 1965 season. A media report after the sixth game of the year indicated Howard had eclipsed the 1,000 yard barrier for the season. One more game was played after the sixth game, but no rushing totals were published in the American Press news article. JT Smith was a true, dual threat quarterback and was credited with a number of rushing and passing scores in the season. Leon Madria was singled out as a defensive standout in the 65 season. The Lions continued their dominance over Carver and their season once again featured a contest against Wiergate in East Texas. The season ended at home in the first week of November. Carl Howard was signed to play for Grambling State University.

Game Notes

| | |
|---|---|
| Carver (DeRidder) | Carl Howard 2 TDs, including 92 yarder, 100+ yards |
| St Matthew | Carl Howard 210 yards rushing, Herbert Burns 120 yards, JT Smith TD pass |
| Grand Avenue (Dequincy) | Carl Howard and JT Smith scored TDs |
| Plaisance | Carl Howard 2 TDs, 180 Yards; 1021 on season |
| Carver (Bunkie) | Carl Howard 92 yd TD catch from Smith; Leon Madria 12 tackles |
| Mossville | Carl Howard 1 TD, JT Smith 1 TD |
| Wiergate | Carl Howard 2 rushing TDs; JT Smith, 1 rushing, 1 passing TD |

# Howard And Co. Stop Carver

Carl Howard showed once again why he's considered one of Louisiana's most exciting football players. So far this year, Vernon has scored 26 points in two ball games and Howard has scored all of the points with the exception of one extra point.

The Lions whipped Carver Saturday night 13-0 and Howard showed his stuff again.

Vernon scored one touchdown in the first quarter as Howard skirted left end and hit pay dirt from 21 yards out. The point after, was missed. In the second quarter, quarterback J. T. Smith was nailed on the 8 yard line following a booming punt to the Lions five yard line. After two running plays failed to net a first down, quarterback Smith called on Howard again and this time Howard caught a Carver linebacker out of position and literally outran the rest of Carver's defenders to score standing up, a 92 yard touchdown gallop, the longest in his career. The P. A. T. was good as Smith hit Spencer.

The Eagles were tough in the second half and didn't allow the Lions to score again. Vernon's young but game defensive unit gave a good account of themselves. Defensive end Leon Madria and Linebacker Murkle Sibley led the defense. The Eagles were stopped everytime they tried to turn Madria's end. Sibley made up for last weeks errors by making and assisting in 12 tackles. He also intercepted an Eagle pass.

The Lions will host the St. Matthew Tigers this Saturday, Sept. 18, 1965 at Wampus Cat Stadium. Game time, 7:30 p.m.

# Vernon Rolls Over St. Mathew 33-7

Carl Howard averaged 30 yards a try Saturday night as Vernon routed the St. Mathew Panthers by 33-7.

Howard scored four touchdowns, the shortest a 40-yard gallop, and gained 210 yards on only seven carries. Hebert Burns turned in another fine offensive game, netting 120 yards in 10 tries.

Vernon's other touchdown came on a 30-yard pass from J. T. Smith

to Alfred Spencer.

attack.

Standout linemen for the Lions were Sylvester Tinsley, Alvoy Wilson, Hilton Wesley, freshmen Lee Bunsh, Melvin Puckett, Michael Mallet and Anton Haynes.

At 7:30 Friday night, Vernon will host DeQuincy's Grand Avenue Tigers for the district championship.

| | | | | |
|---|---|---|---|---|
| St. Mathews | 0 | 0 | 7— | 7 |
| Vernon | 0 | 20 | 0 | 13—33 |

October 9, 1965

# Howard-Led Vernon Runs By Plaisance

LEESVILLE — Carl Howard scored two touchdowns and gained 180 yards rushing to spark the Vernon Lions to a 13-7 victory over the Plaisance Lions here Friday night.

Howard's 180 yards, garnered in 12 trips, ran his season's total rushing mark to 1,021 yards in six games.

He scored touchdowns in the second and third periods to give the Lions a 13-0 lead until the final period when Henry Jackson scored for Plaisance on a three-yard run. Jackson ran across for the extra point.

Howard's first tally was a 20-yard run and his second came on a 46-yard pass play. John Smith passed to Roy Robinson for the extra point.

| | | | | | |
|---|---|---|---|---|---|
| Plaisance | 0 | 0 | 0 | 7— | 7 |
| Vernon | 0 | 6 | 7 | 0—13 | |

V—Carl Howard 20 run. Run failed.
V—Carl Howard 46 pass from John Smith. John Smith pass from Roy Robinson.
P—Henry Jackson 3 run. Henry Jackson run.

# Howard, Lions Nip Bunkie Team

Carl Howard used his blockers well as he led the Vernon Lions past the Carver Eagles (Bunkie) 12-6 Saturday evening.

Howard got the Lions rolling late in the first quarter as he took a pass from quarterback J. T. Smith on the Lions' 15 yard line. Howard was hit but shook off the defender and raced 85 yards to score standing up. The PAT failed as end Leon Madria took the pass out of the end zone.

The half ended with Vernon holding a scant 6-0 lead. The third quarter saw the Eagles score their only tally as they recovered a Lion fumble deep in Lion's territory. Halfback Joe Taylor capped the drive by diving over from the 1 yard line. The conversion failed.

The Lions took over in the fourth quarter to score the final tally. Ralph Lee sneaked over from the two yard line. The point after failed as Smith was short with a pass to end Glenn Garner. The final Lions score was set up following the excellent running of Ralph Lee, Howard and Smith. Lee got 45 yards on six carries.

Defensive end Leon Madria was credited with 12 individual tackles and Smith had eight tackles and one interception.

They will travel to Mossville Oct. 30 for their next game.

# Mossville Out To Stop Carl Howard

MOSSVILLE — Stop Carl Howard!

That's the battle cry for the Mossville Pirates Saturday night when they play host to Howard and his Vernon Lion teammates for a 7:30 p.m. game at West Lake Stadium.

Mossville, beset by schedule problems all season, will be looking for its second victory of the season in this one. The Pirates have lost two.

Vernon has the best record in the area. The Lions stand 3-1 on the season.

Mossville coach LaSalle Williams makes no bones about what must be done to beat Vernon.

"We have to stop Howard," the veteran coach says flatly. "He's the hub of their offense. If we can shut him off, we feel we can beat them.

"We've been fortunate in containing him in the past," Williams continued. "He has not scored on us in three previous games, but with him, you can't let up."

Howard, the object of all this attention is the area's leading scorer, having tallied 54 points in the four games.

A quick, agile runner, he is even more remarkable in that he does it with one arm. His other has been amputated just below the shoulder.

Despite having lost ace fullback Leemon Shankle for the season, the Pirates will not be without some punch of their own.

John Reado, a 255-pound former tackle, will operate at the vacated fullback post. Backing him up will be John Peters, a 192-pounder.

# Pirates Nip Vernon By 14-13 Score

WEST LAKE — The Mossville Pirates edged out the Vernon Lions Saturday night, 14-13.

John Reabo was the work horse for the Pirates scoring both touchdowns and the crucial extra point.

Charles Drake and Mack Bellfessol starred defensively for the Pirates. They collected 28 individual tackles between them, 14 each.

Mossville is now 2-2 and Vernon is 4-3 for the season.

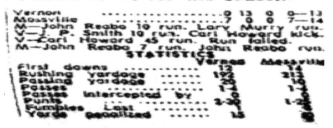

```
Vernon ....................0 13 0 0—13
Mossville ................7 0 0 7—14
M—John Reabo 10 run. Lary Murry run.
V—J. P. Smith 10 run. Carl Howard kick.
V—Carl Howard 45 run. Run failed.
M—John Reabo 7 run. John Reabo run.
                    STATISTICS
                              Vernon  Mossville
First downs ............  12      14
Rushing yardage ......  192      211
Passing yardage ......   20       10
Passes ...............   1        1
Passes intercepted by  2-30     1-2
Punts ................
Fumbles Lost .........
Yards penalized ......   15
```

32

# Vernon In 28-12 Win

LEESVILLE — The Vernon Lions came from behind in the second half for a 28-12 homecoming victory over Wiergate, Tex., here Saturday night.

Down 12-6 at halftime, the Lions got two touchdowns and a safety in the third period and a clinching score in the fourth.

Carl Howard scored twice for the Lions, going two yards in the opening period and 20 yards in the third. Quarterback John Ford plunged for one score and threw 8 yards to Alfred Spencer for another.

Gus Ford scored both of the Texans' touchdowns.

```
Wiergate ............... 6  6  0  0—12
Vernon ................. 6  0 15  7—28
```
W—Gus Ford 3 run. Run failed.
V—Carl Howard 2 run. Run failed.
W—Gus Ford 4 run. Run failed.
V—John Smith 2 run. Run failed.
V—Carl Howard 20 run. Howard run.
V—Safety, Ford tackled in end zone.
V—Alfred Spencer 8 pass from Smith. Smith run.

# Mossville Opens Playoffs Friday

Mossville opens a bid for the Class AA championship a n d W. O. Boston puts the wraps on its regular season before going into the Class AAA playoffs in a pair of Friday night games this week.

Mossville travels to Thibodaux to meet C. M. Washington in the bi-zone playoffs. Mossville captured the District 1-AA crown with a 2-0 record.

Boston takes on Paul Breaux here with no real w o r r i e s about the district title.

Boston, with a 3-0 l e a g u e record, has the title won regardless of the outcome Friday night. Breaux hasn't won a district game, while Washington and Henderson each have a loss and a tie.

The Panthers' Percy F o r e man took over the scoring lead last week, running his season total to 72 points to overhaul Vernon's Carl Howard, who now ranks second with 59.

# Pokes, USL To Decide GSC Title

**GULF STATES CONFERENCE**

| Conference Games | W | L | T | Pct. | TP | OP |
|---|---|---|---|---|---|---|
| McNeese | 4 | 0 | 0 | 1.000 | 75 | 40 |
| Southwestern | 3 | 1 | 0 | .750 | 81 | 38 |
| Southeastern | 2 | 2 | 0 | .500 | 49 | 34 |
| La. Tech | 2 | 2 | 0 | .500 | 82 | 64 |
| Northwestern | 1 | 3 | 0 | .250 | 59 | 124 |
| Northeast | 0 | 4 | 0 | .000 | 34 | 59 |

| All Games | W | L | T | Pct. | TP | OP |
|---|---|---|---|---|---|---|
| Southwestern | 6 | 2 | 0 | .750 | 134 | 51 |
| McNeese | 5 | 3 | 0 | .625 | 100 | 116 |
| Southeastern | 4 | 3 | 0 | .571 | 86 | 63 |
| Northwestern | 4 | 4 | 0 | .500 | 133 | 167 |
| La. Tech | 3 | 4 | 0 | .479 | 107 | 115 |
| Northeast | 1 | 6 | 0 | .143 | 51 | 140 |

**THE REMAINING SCHEDULE**
SATURDAY: xMcNeese at Southwestern, xNortheast at La. Tech, xNorthwestern at Southeastern.
NOV. 25: Southwestern at Chattanooga.
NOV. 27: Appalachian State at Southeastern.

**THE SCORING LEADERS**

| | TD | FG | PAT | TP |
|---|---|---|---|---|
| Walet, McNeese | 8 | 0 | 0 | 48 |
| Walker, NW | 0 | 5 | 16 | 31 |

**TRI-PARISH NEGRO**

| | W | L | T | Pct. | TP | OP |
|---|---|---|---|---|---|---|
| W. O. Boston | 8 | 1 | 0 | .889 | 196 | 37 |
| Vernon | 4 | 2 | 0 | .667 | 114 | 51 |
| Gr. Avenue | 6 | 2 | 0 | .750 | 106 | 64 |
| Mossville | 4 | 2 | 0 | .667 | 123 | 64 |
| Washington | 2 | 5 | 1 | .313 | 138 | 39 |
| Carver | 0 | 7 | 1 | .111 | 34 | 138 |

**THIS WEEK'S SCHEDULE**
FRIDAY: Paul Breaux at B o s t o n, Mossville vs. Washington at Thibodaux, B Zone playoff.

**SCORING LEADERS**

| | TD | PAT | TP |
|---|---|---|---|
| Foreman, Boston | 12 | 0 | 72 |
| Howard, Vernon | 9 | 5 | 59 |
| Sims, Gr.Ave. | 8 | 1 | 49 |
| Gatson, Wash. | 7 | 0 | 42 |
| Davis, Mossville | 6 | 0 | 36 |
| Abram, Gr. Ave. | 5 | 3 | 33 |

33

# 1966

The season in 1966 saw a changing of the guard and a transition from the remaining players from the 63 team to a group that would dominate in ensuing years.   Quarterback JT Smith was at the helm for another year, and a group of younger players also emerged to carry on the Lion Tradition.   Information on some of the games in 1966 remains obscure.   Though a pre-season schedule was uncovered, several of the games were not recorded in the media in any location.

| Game Date | W | L | | | | | |
|---|---|---|---|---|---|---|---|
| 2-Sep | | L | Vernon | 0 | Mansfield | 30 | |
| 9-Sep | W | | Vernon | 39 | Carver (DeRidder) | 0 | |
| 16-Sep | | L | Vernon | 13 | Melrose | 20 | |
| 1-Oct | W | | Vernon | | Sabine (Many) | | |
| 7-Oct | W | | Vernon | 7 | Plaisance | 2 | |
| 15-Oct | W | | Vernon | 13 | Carver (Bunkie) | 6 | |
| 21-Oct | | L | Vernon | 0 | Grand Avenue (Dequincy) | 7 | |
| 28-Oct | | L | Vernon | 19 | Mossville | 38 | |
| 3-Nov | | | Vernon | | Wiergate | | |
| | 5 | 4 | | | | | |

Game Notes

| Mansfield | Vida Blue QB for DeSoto High; Michael Mallet 79 yards passing and 100 yard rushing for VHS |
|---|---|
| Carver (DeRidder) | TDs by Marvin Foster, Lemon Johnson, Michael Mallet, Don Mallet |
| Melrose | Ralph Lee and Calvin Jones scored TDs |
| Sabine (Many) | Second half comeback win; no media reporting discovered; personal accounts |
| Plaisance | No game notes discovered |
| Carver (Bunkie) | 100 yds rushing by JT Smith; TD by Leonard Johnson; Roy Robinson TD pass to Leon Madria |
| Grand Avenue (Dequincy) | No game notes discovered |
| Mossville | Lemon Johnson, TD run; JT Smith TD run and pass (to Johnson) |
| Wiergate | Probably lost; media reporting from Texas indicates Wiergate went undefeated in up through the state championship in early Dec 1966 |

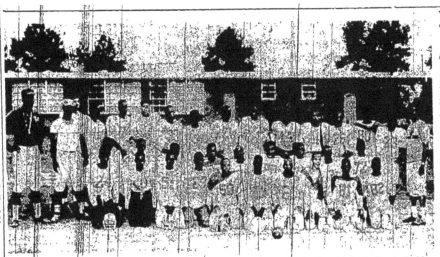

VERNON HIGH SCHOOL LIONS are young and eager, but they got off to a bad start this year, dropping their opener in Lake Charles during the last few seconds of a game played August 27. The team consists of first row (from left): Milton Wesley, Elmo Jackson, Wade Garner, J. T. Buckley, Shelton Quiney, Hilton Wesley, Ernest Sawyer, Thomas Ellis, Thaddeus Rowe, and Joe Lee Drain. Second row (from left): Foster Thomas, head coach; Murphy Fish-

er, assistant coach; Donald Rock, Lewis Smith, Albert Haynes, Mose Tinsley, Calvin Wilson, Sherry Thomas, Leonard Johnson, Arthur Ellis and Melvin Dotson. Back row (from left): Charles Richards, J. T. Smith, Donald Mallet, Antonne Haynes, Marvin Foster, Ralph Lee, Michael Mallet, Leon Madria, Henry Jackson, Leandrea Bursh, LeRoy Jackson, Sonny Wallace, Roy Robinson and Samuel Bursh, assistant coach.

Staff Photo

## Vernon Fielding Young Team This Season

With two weeks of hard work behind them, the Vernon High Lions opened the 1966 Football season in Lake Charles, when they lost 6-0 to Grand Avenue High School of DeQuincy in the Annual Jamboree.

Head Coach Foster Thomas said that the Lions are very young this year, with a squad of 33, only nine lettermen returning. Also the Lions are smaller than usual.

With the determination that the young Lions have already shown we should have a favorable season.

### FOOTBALL SCHEDULE

| Sept. 2 | Mansfield | There |
| Sept. 9 | DeRidder | Here |
| Sept. 16 | Melrose | There |
| Sept. 23 | Open | |
| Oct. 1 | Many | There |
| Oct. 7 | Plaisance | There |
| Oct. 15 | Bunkie | Here |
| Oct. 21 | DeQuincy | There |
| Oct. 28 | Mossville | Here |
| Nov. 3 | Weirgate | There |

All Homes games start at 7:30 P. M.

---

## THURSDAY, SEPTEMBE 8, 1966 -

### Vernon Drops Opener To Triple A DeSoto Team

The Vernon Lions found themselves on the short end of a David-Goliath Battle as they faced the DeSoto High School's all-state quarterback Vider Blue who called the signals behind a line which averaged 217 lbs. The class "A" Lions dropped their season opener 3-0 to Class "AAA" DeSoto High School of Mansfield. Blue accounted for four of DeSoto's five T. D.'s as he passed for three and scored on an eight yard run, and also accounted for three PAT's.

Young Sophomore Michael Mallet rose to the challenge of his first assignment as full-time Quarterback for the Lions as he accounted for all the Lions yards rushing and passing. Mike connected on four of ten passes for a total of seventy nine yards and a spectacular 116 yards on four carries for an average of 29 yards per carry, rushing.

The Lions will host Carver High School of DeRidder Friday Sept. 9, 7:30 p.m. at Wampus Cat Stadium in their first home game of the season. Friday night is "Parent's Night" for the Lions who will be seeking to stretch their fine season streak over Carver to six.

35

# Vernon tops Carver in scoring spree

LEESVILLE — The Vernon Lions and Carver Eagles staged a scoring contest in the first game of the 1966 season for both teams, with Vernon coming out on top of the heap, 39-20, here Friday night.

Vernon jumped off to a quick 13-0 lead after the first quarter as Marvin Foster and Calvin Wilson carried the pigskin in from the four and seven-yard line, respectively. Leonard Johnson ran over the extra point after the first score.

The Lions again drew blood in the second stanza as Mike Mallet scored from the two and passed to Don Mallet for the point after touchdown, but Carver marched right back with Bluitt McMahon scoring on a three-yard plunge.

Johnson returned a punt 59 yards to open the scoring for the Lions in the second half before McMahon put Carver back on the scoreboard with a 60-yard run to make the score, 27-13.

Mike Mallet and Ralph Lee sewed up the Vernon victory with runs of 13 and 10 yards, respectively. Ralph McMahon rounded out the scoring taking a 61-yard pass from Bluitt McMahon.

Carver ............... 6 7 13
Vernon ............... 13 7 13

V—Marvin Foster 4 run. Leonard Johnson run.
V—Calvin Wilson 7 run. Run failed.
V—Mike Mallet 2 run. Don Mallet pass from Mike Mallet.
C—Bluitt McMahon 3 run. Run failed.
C—Leonard Johnson 59 punt return. Run failed.
C—Bluitt McMahon 60 run. Bluitt McMahon run.
V—Mike Mallet 13 run. Pass failed.
V—Ralph Lee 10 run. Leonard Johnson run.
C—Ralph McMahon 61 pass from Bluitt McMahon. McMahon run.

STATISTICS

# Vernon Lions drop 20-13 decision

MELROSE — Melrose quarterback Lloyd Jones ran and passed the Melrose Tigers to a 20-13 victory over Vernon of Leesville here Friday afternoon.

Jones scored twice, on runs of 54 and five yards, ran for two extra points, had 123 yards rushing and connected on four of eight passes for 57 yards to steal the show.

Vernon meanwhile was able to hit on only one of 12 passes and fumbled the ball away three times.

Vernon ................ 7 0 6 0—13
Melrose ............... 7 6 7 0—20
M—Lloyd Jones 54 run. Lloyd Jones run.
V—Calvin Wilson 15 run. Leonard Johnson.
M—Earl Helarie 6 run. Run failed.
V—Ralph Lee 41 run. Run failed.
M—Lloyd Jones 5 run. Lloyd Jones run.

STATISTICS

# Grand Avenue beats Vernon

DEQUINCY — Jerry Carter ran a punt back 40 yards to give the Grand Avenue Tigers a 7-0 victory over Vernon High Lions Saturday night.

Robert Monroe carried the ball nine times for an average of nine yards per carry. Elisjah Stevenson added 43 yards on the ground.

Randolph Pinkney and Claibon Skinner were standouts on defense with nine tackles each.

```
Vernon ................ 0  0  0  0— 0
Grand Avenue .......... 0  0  7  0— 7
```
GA—Jerry Carter 40 punt return. Robert Monroe run.

## STATISTICS

|  | Vernon | Grand Ave. |
|---|---|---|
| First downs | 17 | 17 |
| Rushing yardage | 206 | 208 |
| Passing yardage | 30 | 0 |
| Passes | 0-1 | 4-9 |
| Passes Intercepted by | 0 | 0 |
| Punts | 3-30 | 3-35 |
| Fumbles lost | 1 | 0 |
| Yards penalized | 50 | 50 |

# Vernon strikes late for victory over Bunkie, 13-6

LEESVILLE — The Vernon Lions pushed over a touchdown in each of the last two quarters to record a 13-6 victory over Carver High of Bunkie here Saturday night.

J. T. Smith was the workhorse for Vernon with 106 yards on 11 carries.

```
Carver ................ 6  0  0  0— 6
Vernon ................ 0  0  7  6—13
```
C—Willie McGee 3 run. Run failed.
V—Leonard Johnson 5 run. J. T. Smith run.
V—Leon Madria 5 pass from Roy Robinson. Run failed.

## STATISTICS

|  | Carver | Vernon |
|---|---|---|
| First downs | 17 | 19 |
| Rushing yardage | 126 | 267 |
| Passing yardage | 78 | 41 |
| Passes | 9-15 | 2-7 |
| Passes intercepted by | 0 | 3 |
| Punts | 1-33 | 6-47 |
| Fumbles lost | 0 | 0 |
| Yards penalized | 30 | 35 |

## It's Homecoming Time At Vernon High

Vernon High School is observing its annual homecoming this week with a number of activities.

Along with the normal weekly activities, the Saturday activity will open at 6:30 a.m. with a Father-Son Breakfast for the Vernon Lions, sponsored by the Quarterback Club. There will be a parade at 2 p.m. At 7:30 p.m. the Lions will host the Carver High School Eagles of Bunkie, followed by the Annual Homecoming Dance in the school gym.

The Lions defeated the Eagles last season 18-6 and are just back from a 7-2 victory over the Indians of Plaisance.

## Pirates come from behind for victory

LEESVILLE — The Mossville Pirates ruined the Vernon Lion homecoming activities as the Pirates pummeled the Lions, 38-19, here Friday night.

The Pirates, however, had to come from behind in the third period to mark the victory. At intermission, Vernon led 19-13 with all the Lion markers coming in the second frame.

Mossville notched the first two scores, but Vernon got three in a row to push the Pirates back.

The final half was all Mossville work, as the Pirates scored four times.

Mossville now has a 2-5 record in season play to Vernon's 4-4 overall mark.

Scoring for Mossville on long plays were Charles Ross who ran an intercepted pass back 85 yards for a score and Charles Drake who ran from scrimmage for 85 yards and a marker. Ross Cate got the first Mossville touchdown after the half with a sprint of 45 yards with an intercepted pass.

Mossville .................. 7  6 12 13—38
Vernon ...................... 0 19  0  0—19
M—Howard Green 2 run. Charles Drake run.
M—Barry Edwards 1 run. Run failed.
V—Lemon Johnson 4 run. Run failed.
V—Lemon Johnson 4 pass from J. T. Smith. Kick failed.
V—J. T. Smith 2 run. J. T. Smith run.
M—Ross Cate 45 pass interception. Run failed.
M—Charles Ross 85 pass interception. Kick failed.
M—Charles Drake 85 run. Kick failed.
M—Charles Drake 4 run. Howard Green run.

38

# 1967:  Back to the Championship

The Vernon High School Lions stormed through the 1967 season without a loss.   The final season record is listed at 8-0-1.    The Lions tied in the first week of the season but suffered no other blemishes on their record for the entire year.   Wins against annual rivals Wiergate, Mossville, and Grand Avenue were accompanied by a road win against Grambling High in Lincoln Parish and a playoff win in Denham Springs.    VHS played Good Pine twice during the year, once in the season, and in the title game.    Key players on the squad were Leonard Johnson, Michael (Mike) Mallet, Calvin Wilson, and Leroy Jackson.

| Game Date | W | L | Tie | | | | | |
|-----------|---|---|-----|---|---|---|---|---|
| 14-Sep | | | 1 | Vernon | 7 | Carver (Bunkie) | | 7 |
| 21-Sep | W | | | Vernon | 35 | St. Matthew | | 0 |
| 28-Sep | W | | | Vernon | 65 | Good Pine | | 0 |
| 5-Oct | W | | | Vernon | 34 | Wiergate | | 0 |
| 12-Oct | W | | | Vernon | 13 | Grambling | | 12 |
| 20-Oct | W | | | Vernon | 42 | Grand Avenue (Dequincy) | | 0 |
| 8-Nov | W | | | Vernon | 13 | Mossvile | | 0 |
| 16-Nov | W | | | Vernon | 33 | West Livingston | | 6 |
| 7-Dec | W | | | Vernon | 27 | Good Pine | | 0 |
| | 8 | 0 | 1 | | | | | |

Of note in the 1967 season was a 14-year old freshman, Donnie Gilbert being thrust into the spotlight as the Lions' starting quarterback.   The regular starter, Michael Mallet, was sidelined due to an injury, and his backup had been dismissed from the team.   Gilbert, at 14 years of age, got his first start in the playoff game and led the Lions to wins at West Livingston and in the title game against Good Pine.

Game Notes

| | |
|---|---|
| Good Pine | Leonard Johnson, Michael Mallet, Louis Hopkins, Marvin Foster scored TDs |
| Wiergate | Leonard Johnson 68 yd TD run, Marvin Johnson, TDs |
| Grambling | Leonard Johnson 83 yd punt return TD; Johnson 71 yard TD pass to Leon Madria |
| Grand Avenue (Dequincy) | Leonard Johnson 172 yards rushing; Marvin Foster 71 yards; |
| Mossvile | No game report discovered |
| W. Livingston (Denham Springs) | Calvin Wilson 213 yards rushing, 3 TDs; Donnie Gilbert 3 x TD passes |
| Good Pine | Calvin Wilson, 178 yards rushing, 3 TDs; 127 yard receiving, 3 INTs |

## Vernon Cuts Down Goodpine, 65-0

The Vernon High Lions finally had a chance to show off their talents to the homefolk after two consecutive game cancellations by their opponents, and the young Lions let go with everything they had in defeating last year's State runner-ups, 65-0.

The Lions cleaned their bench in using twenty-nine of its thirty man roster and everything they put onto the field looked good.

Coach Foster Thomas, however, seems a little less optimistic than the average spectator as he looks forward to Friday night's clash with the Wiergate Panters, last years Texas State Champs.

To quote Coach Thomas, "then we'll really have an opportunity to see what we've got. We'll probably have to go with our very best right down to the wire with no room for error".

In Saturday night's run-a-way, the Lions scored ten touchdowns and five points after to establish a school record of sixty-five points.

SCORING:
V—Leonard Johnson ......37 yd. run
PAT run failed
V—Michael Mallet ..... 12 yd. run
PAT Lewis Smith—Kick
V—Marvin Smith ......... 6 yd. run
PAT—Lewis Smith—Kick
V—Michael Mallet ......10 yd. run
PAT—Lewis Smith—Kick
V—Louis Hopkins .,,......7 yd. run
PAT—Kick – failed
V—Marvin Foster ........55 yd. run
PAT—Mallet pass to Leon Madria
V—21 yd. pass from Mallet to Madria
PAT—Kick failed
V—Mallet ...................7 yd. run
PAT—Kick failed
V—Leonard Johnson ..... 31 yd. run
PAT – pass failed
V—Foster .............. 11 yd. run
PAT—Louis Smith—Kick

SCORE BY QUARTERS:
Vernon ................26  20  6  13
Good Pine .............0   0   0  0

## Vernon Tames Texan '11'

The Vernon High School Lions continued their winning ways as Coach Foster Thomas sent his charges to their second consecutive win against no loses. The Lions played host Friday to Wiergate High School of Texas who were Texas state champions last season, and promptly started the score board clicking.

Wiergate won the coin toss and elected to receive and after being held to a punting situation, surrendered the ball to the Lions who sent Leonard Johnson for a 61 yard scamper off tackle for the T.D. Mallet converted and the Lions quickly regained possession of the ball. A few more ticks of the clock and Marvin Foster, Lions fullback went through the middle for a 5 yard T. D. Louis Smith then kicked his first of two points after touchdown and sent the Lions ahead 14-0 at the end of the first stanza. The Lions went on to score in every quarter for their 34-0 victory.

The Lions brought their two game scoring total to 99 points while holding their opponents scoreless.

When asked about individual performers, Coach Thomas gave his reply "Take your pick. The average spectator knows that our backs and ends are above average but what they never see is that interior line. We have five boys from tackle to tackle that I wouldn't trade for all the backs in the world. Very few spectators know them by their numbers because they never come off the field—they're "60 minute men".

The Lions travel to Grambling Friday for battle with the Grambling High School Cubs. The Lions next home appearance will be October 21 when they take on the Grand Ave. Tigers of DeQuincy for Homecoming and the zone 1, District 1 championship all in one package.

# Vernon Edges By Grambling, 13-12

The Vernon High Lions came from behind to edge the Grambling High Cubs 13-12. The Lions trailed 12-0 at half-time intermission after the cubs scored 6 points in each of the first two periods on plays of 14 and 39 yd passes from Gerald McNeal to Cecil Gray, but failed to convert for the points after touchdowns. In the meantime Vernon seemed to find no holes in the stubborn Grambling defense.

The Lions, however, reversed the action after going over the Grambling defense at intermission and ironing out a few wrinkles of their own.

The Lions struck early in the third stanza when Leonard Johnson, Vernon halfback took a punt on the Vernon 17 yd line and went the 83 yard distance for the first Vernon score. Vernon failed to convert on a bad snap from center.

Vernon's next touchdown came with less than three minutes remaining when Leonard Johnson found Leon Madria on the other end of a pass which went for 71 yds. The pass went for 23 yds in the air and the 6'4" co-captain had a chance to show off his blinding speed which has won the attention of cinder fans throughout the state, and he did just that. Louis Smith then kicked the point after to send the Lions ahead 13-12.

Smith put the game on ice with a spectacular one-hand interception to give Vernon the ball with time running out.

The Lions face Grand Avenue High School of DeQuincy at Wampus Cat Stadium October 21 in their annual Homecoming and District 1, Zone 11, L. I. A. L. O. championship game.

41

# Vernon Wins District Title With 42-0 Homecoming Triumph Over Tigers

Vernon High School won its annual homecoming game 42-0 over the Grand Avenue Tigers of De-Quincy Saturday night and at the same time won the District 1, Zone 1, class A championship.

The potent Lion's offense scored in every period of play while the stubborn defense never allowed itself to get into serious trouble. Only once late in the fourth period did the Tigers pose a threat but the Lions held for four consecutive plays on their own 12 yard line even though the regular defense was on the bench watching their possible successors.

When asked about outstanding players, Coach Thomas gave in his usual solemn manner, "I could give you about 12 or 13 names of most valuable players tonight." In the backfield, halfback Leonard Johnson sparkled with three touchdowns of 2, 12 and 44 yard runs, he picked up 172 yards rushing in 16 carries for an average of 10.75 yards per carry, caught two Michael Mallet passes for a total of 57 yards, and returned two De-Quincy punts for a total of 76 yards. Yet, the clutch running of senior fullback Marvin Foster cannot be overlooked. Foster rushed for 71 yards in 13 carries picking up seven first downs.

Leon Madria, who played the entire ballgame under double and tripple coverage did an excellent job as a decoy receiver. He always had two or three men far down the field and out of play. Double coverage, however, was not enough when the lanky end ran the "end around" for a 15 yard T. D.

The interior line play, both offensive and defensive, however, tells the success story for the Lions this season. Henry Jackson, Earnest Sawyer, Hilton Wesley, and Cecil Woods, all juniors, played their usual magnificent game. "The play of these four boys", commented Coach Thomas, "is reflected in the fact that we have scored 161 points in five games while allowing the opposition only 19 points".

The Lions next travel to Westlake to take on the Moosville Pirates Friday at Ram Stadium in Westlake.

42

HILTON WESLEY AND Michael Mallet (on ground) tackle a Grand Avenue runner. Identifiable Vernon High players are (23) Glover Carter, Hilton Wesley, Henry Jackson and Leon Ma-dria. Vernon rambled past the DeQuincy team, 42-0.

—Photo by Earl Jackson

LEONARD JOHNSON (20) finds plenty of running room as Cecil Woods (51) and Henry Jackson (70) look for someone to block. On the ground at right is Hilton Wesley who has just opened the way for Johnson.

—Photo by Earl Jackson

Quarterback Michael Mallet

Richwood (Monroe) 39, Richardson (West Monroe) 0

Carroll (Monroe) 32, Peabody (Alexandria) 0

Morehouse (Bastrop) 25, Eastside (Farmerville) 6

B. T. Washington (Shreveport) 30, Capitol (Baton Rouge) 13

Princeton 13, Eden Gardens (Shreveport) 0

Valencia (Shreveport) 39, Central (Natchitoches) 12

Washington (Lake Charles) 57, J. S. Clark (Opelousas) 0

Vernon (Leesville) 13, Mossville 0

Thursday, November 16, 1967

# Vernon Lions In Class A Finals

Vernon High School defeated West Livingston High School of Denham Springs 32-6 to cinch a playoff with Goodpine High School of Trout for the L. I. A. L. O. class "A" state championship.

Gilbert, however, is the first to admit that he didn't do it alone. He quickly pointed out clutch plays which were suggested to him by halfback Calvin Wilson, and he brags "I had the best line in class "A" football in front of me only once was I trapped behind the line for a loss".

Wilson had his best game of the year against the Trojans in running three touchdowns of 21, 14, and 37 yds., and picking up 213 yds. rushing to set a season high in that department.

Vernon will face Goodpine Thursday, November 16, at 7:30 p.m. in Trout.

———(0———)

45

DECEMBER 7, 1967

# Lions Are 'A' Champs

The Vernon High School Lions defeated Goodpine High School of Trout 26-0 to win their second state championship in five years.

The Thursday night game brought the Class 'A' football competition to a close for 1967.

Already coach Thomas is looking forward to next year.

"We only have two seniors," he grins, and our freshman crew showed a lot of promise this year.

Goodpine won the coin toss and commeced to make it look like a ball game. The Lions defense finally rose up and halted them at the Vernon 29.

Goodpine stayed in control most of the first quarter, but the second stanza was all Vernon as the classy Lions banged over three touchdowns.

I. T. Grant ran 15 yards for for one score and Marvin Foster tallied on a five yard jaunt. Calvin Lewis, a 9.8 sprinter broke loose following Foster's score and zipped 41 yards to score the third TD of the quarter.

Louis Smith 'icked one extra point.

Vernon wrapped up the scoring by shoving over a third period touchdown.

The Leesville team finished the season with a record of 8-0-1. In those nine games, Vernon compiled 362 points to 44 by opponents.

In junior halfback Calvin Wilson, the Lions have a seemingly sure-fire all-state candidate.

In the playoffs alone, Wilson socerd six touchdowns, picked up 14 first downs, rushed for 391 yards, caught six passes for 127 and returned three intercepted passes for 63 yards. He also averaged 19.3 yards on punt returns.

This week at Vernon, the boys aren't resting on their news clippings—they all showed up Friday for basketball practice.

VERNON HIGH LIONS
1967
STATE A CHAMPS
FOOTBALL

SHOWN ABOVE is the Vernon High Lions Class 'A' champion-ship team. Helping the Lions compiled an 8-0-1 record were these players: Front row, Jimmie Calvin, J. T. Buckley, Ralph Scott, Milton Wesley, Donnie Gilbert, Hilton Wesley, Jerry Haynes, Joe Drain, Louis Hopkins, Thomas Martin, Jimmy Haynes. Second row: Julius Richard, Bobby Thomas, Freddie Davis, Johnny Martin, Don Woods, Hosie Jones, Gary Johnson, Jerry Coin, Jerry Brown, Willie Garner, Marvin Foster, Calvin Wilson. Third row: Leonard Johnson, Mose Tinsley, Henry Jackson, Sherry Thomas, Sonny Wallace, Leon Madria, Michael Mallet, Louis Smith, Charles Rich-chard, and Issac Grant. Also shown are principal Fletcher Cheat-ham, and coaches Samuel Bursh, Foster Thomas, and James Fi-sher.

—Photo by Earl Jackson

CALVIN WILSON

EARNEST SAWYER

47

# State  Champs

**FOSTER THOMAS**
Head Coach

MURPHY FISHER
Defensive Coach

SAMUEL BURSH
Offensive Coach

JOSEPH DEAMER
Defensive Coach

Quarterback Donnie Gilbert

L-R: Mose Tinsley, Earnest Sawyer, Thomas Martin

## 1968:  Third Title, Most Wins In A Season

The Lions of the 1968 season achieved more wins than any other Vernon team, running the table undefeated and finishing the year as undefeated state champions with a 10-0 record. The squad from VHS was led by star quarterback Michael Mallet, who would go on to coaching fame at Leesville and LSU in the coming years.   Other Lion standouts for the year were Louis Johnson, Louis Hopkins, Leonard Johnson and Donnie Gilbert.

Media reporting from 1968 was limited to non-existent.   In the search for results, only two game articles were uncovered.  One was from the playoff game versus Buergher, and the other was from the state title game, against old foe Good Pine.

## THURSDAY, NOVEMBER 28, 1968

### Vernon Lions Grab District Pigskin Title

The Vernon High Lions came from behind to win a 19-7 victory over the Burgher High Tigers of Independence, November 9.

The first score came late in the first quarter when the Lions' Leonard Johnson intercepted a screen pass and carried the pigskin 35-yards for a TD.

The point after attempt by Mike Mallet went wide to the right. The quarter ended with Vernon leading 6-0.

But the Burgher Tigers came back in the second quarter and made their bid for the Crown with a minute and a quarter left in the half. Fullback Curtis Snow took the pitch-out from quarterback John Sanders for a 35-yard end sweep TD run. The point after by Snow gave the Tigers a half time lead over Vernon 7-6.

In the third quarter the Lions gave an indication of their offensive might the first time they had the ball, driving 64-yards in three plays. The payoff came on a finger-tip TD catch by Leonard Johnson. Mike Mallet carried the ball around the end for an extra point, pushing the Lions out front once more, 13-7.

The Vernon Lions' defense was magnificent.

This set up another TD pattern for Vernon on an off-tackle run by Mallet, making the final score 19-7.

The victory insured the undefeated Lions a chance to keep the 1-A State Championship Crown they won last year. The championship game will be played here in Leesville, November 22.

"With the hard work put forth on the boys by our coaches, I feel confident that we will keep that crown at Vernon," said Fletcher Cheatham, principal.

Foster Thomas, head coach for the Vernon Lions, said, "We have a good ball club, but if we want to keep the crown we won last year, we'll have to play a much better ball game than the one we played against Burgher High."

# Lions Retain Class A Title

Leesville's Vernon High School Lions retained the State Class A football crown for the second straight year in an anti-climax 58-0 home tilt against Good Pine High November 22.

The raging Lions of Coach Foster Thomas completed the 1968 circuit with an unblemished slate. In the title game the Lions scored nine times with Leonard Johnson accounting for three, Louis Hopking three; Calvin Wilson, two, and Michael Mallet, one. Points after were chalked up by Johnson, Smith and Hopkins.

Coach Thomas is optomistic about the rebuilding job necessary to counter the loss of 11 starters when he fields next year's squad.

"On the surface it looks bad, but we have a lot of new and promising material with which to work," he said.

"Fortunately, 15 experienced players from this year will be back again for next season. They include players such as Donnie Gilbert, reserve quarterback who did yeoman duty when Coach Thomas' starter was unable to suit up.

Another holdover upon whom Thomas is pinning high hopes is halfback I. T. Grant, called the fastest player in Class A football.

Grant saw little action this year because of an early injury. Others returning: Jerry Haynes, running back. Antone Haynes, end; Henry Jackson, center; Johnny Martin, right tackle, John Buckley, left tackle; Sonny Wallace, end; and Michael Jones. right guard.

"We expect to field another well rounded team in 1969, but it is a little early to make any predictions at this point," Coach Thomas said.

Leroy Jackson, Class of 1969

# 1969: Another Year of Winning

In the aftermath of 1968s's unprecedented 10-0 season, Coach Thomas began the process of creating a new dynasty, and continued the tradiiton of winning.   After losing a great many seniors, the Lions re-loaded with younger talent and kept up their winning ways.   As with 1968, the media reporting in 1969 was less than prolific.   Few if any articles were discovered in media for this research.   The Lions fell to Carlson High of Saint Martinville and lost a two point affair to long time rival Plaisance.   VHS continued their dominance of Carver (DeRidder) and Grand Avenue.

| Game Date | W | L | | | | |
|---|---|---|---|---|---|---|
| 13-Sep | W | | Vernon | 46 | Carver (DeRidder) | 0 |
| 19-Sep | W | | Vernon | | Grambling | |
| 20-Sep | | L | Vernon | 18 | Plaisance | 20 |
| 26-Sep | W | | Vernon | | Burkeville (TX) | |
| 3-Oct | | L | Vernon | 14 | Carlson (Breaux Bridge) | 44 |
| 18-Oct | W | | Vernon | 18 | Grand Avenue (Dequincy) | 6 |
| 25-Oct | | | Vernon | | | |
| | 4 | 2 | | | | |

THURSDAY, SEPTEMBER 11, 1969

# Vernon High Lions will open season here against DeRidder

"We have a ball club that's little in size and experience, but big with desire and guts."

That's the way Head Coach Foster Thomas describes his Vernon High School Lions, who open the 1969 season with Carver High of DeRidder, Saturday night.

"Despite the fact that we lost 15 senior players last year, we feel confident that our fans will still witness a championship team in action Saturday night," said Principal Fletcher Cheatham. "We are looking forward to another successful year."

Vernon High finished first in the 1-A race last year with a 10-0 recored which gave them the 1-A State Championship crown for the second consecutive year.

Kick-off time for the Lions' first season game is 7:30 p. m. at Wampus Cat stadium. Admission is 75 cents for students and $1.25 for adult. Fans may purchase season tickets for $5 by contacting the football coaches and players or call V.H.S. 239-3836, between the hours of 8:15 and 3:15.

"We have only 12 lettermen returning this year," said Coach Thomas, "And with very little preseason practice, they have a big, big job ahead of them." Lettermen include M. Tinsley, M. Jones, S. Wallace, M. Wesley, A. Haynes, D. Gilbert, G. Carter, J. Buckley, G. Johnson, C. Barrow and Sam Johnson.

## VERNON HIGH SCHOOL 1969 FOOTBALL SCHEDULE

| | | |
|---|---|---|
| Sept. 13 | DeRidder | Home |
| Sept. 19 | Grambling High | Away |
| Sept. 26 | Burkeville High (Texas) | Home |
| Oct. 3 | Breaux Bridge | Home |
| Oct. 10 | St. Joseph | Away |
| Oct. 18 | DeQuincy | (Home) Homecoming |
| Oct. 25 | St. Martinville | Home |
| Oct. 31 | Open | Away |
| Nov. 7 | Open | Away |

# Plaisance Meets Vernon High

PLAISANCE — The Plaisance High School Indians go against Vernon High School of Leesville Friday night. The contest will be held at Plaisance High starting at 7:30 p.m.

Coach Hamilton's Indians will be attempting to bounce the Vernon High 11 from the ranks of the unbeaten. The Leesville team, which plays Class AA ball, has gone undefeated in two opening games. Tickets are available at $1.25 and $.75 at the gate.

The AA Indians will attempt to go above the .500 mark for the first time this season. The team dropped its opening contest but then solidly trounced Breaux Bridge 26-0. Hamilton explains that the reorganization of school zones hampered the program a bit but the delays were overcome with some outstanding football players who are willing to give 100 per cent.

Leading the team into battle will be the touchdown twins: Hayward Fontenot Jr. and Nathaniel McCoy.

Fontenot scored a pair of TDs in the team's romp last Friday. He opened the team scoring with a 10-yard jaunt in the first quarter. And then he covered 12 yards and stepped over the goal line for the third TD. Quarterback John Scott did his share of the work as he tallied the team's second marker on a two-yard sneak. His two kicks gave him eight points. The other Plaisance score was recorded on a 15-yard gallop by McCoy.

# Plaisance High Takes 20-18 Victory

PLAISANCE — The Plaisance Indians put a stop to the Vernon High Lions' five year winning streak on Friday night by edging the Lions with a score of 20 to 18. The powerful Lions had defeated DeRidder 46 to 8 in last week's contest while the Indians gave Breaux Bridge a 26 to 0 "spanking".

Vernon High used a combination of a field goal, a T. D. an extra point and a safety to lead the Plaisance Indians by the score of 11 to 0 at the end of the first period of play.

Plaisance quickly stopped the "roar of the Lions" in the second period with Harold Edwards taking a 15 yard pass for a T. D. and Clarence Thierry kicking the extra point. Plaisance reached "paydirt" again in the second quarter when left guard Michael Thierry recovered a fumble for a T. D. Clarence Thierry scored his second extra point to send the

Plaisance Indians into a 14 to 11 halftime lead.

Plaisance's Hayward Fontenot galloped seven yards early in the third period to give the Indians a 20 to eleven commanding lead. The powerful Lions "roared" again in the third period of play with a 10 yard pass to their 6' 6" end. The

Vernon High Lions managed to give the Indians several threats in the fourth period of play, but the Indians defensive unit, known as the "Pythons", used several goal line stands, including a two yard stand, to stop the Lions. Final score: Indians 20 and Lions 18.

Other outstanding offensive

players for the Indians were: Linus Lavergne, Floyd Richard, Nathaniel McCoy and Michael Romar. Clarence Collins, Errol Elliot and Amous Cluse were outstanding on defense.

The Indians will meet Carver High of DeRidder in a District contest at home on Friday. Kickoff time is 7:30 p.m.

# Eunice High Trips 2-AAA Lake Charles

EUNICE — When two football teams play their best game of the season it has to be a whale of a contest. Especially when it involves Double-A and Triple-A teams.

Friday night the Eunice High

confines of Bobcat Field after two road games, and defeated the District 2-AAA Lake Charles team 16-6.

Coach Nagata of the Bobcats stated after the game it was his team's best game of the year

Waller, who was injured last week, was used sparingly carrying just once for four yards. Another Bobcat regular, Jimmy Meeks, was unable to play at guard.

Hamilton attempted 11

55

# Carlson Beats Vernon, 44-14

ST. MARTINVILLE — The Adam Carlson Tigers romped over the Vernon High eleven Friday night in St. Martinville by a 44 - 14 count.

Leading the Carlson attack was the Larry Narcisse to Johnny Mitchell combination which accounted for four Carlson six pointers. Others scoring for the Tigers were Todd Jacket who returned an intercepted pass for 40 yards in the third period and Randy Francois who ran a 25 yard off tackle play in the third period.

Vernon High was paced by the Allen Johnson to Warren Richardson combo. Johnson connected with Richardson on a 45 yarder in the opening period and again on a 15 yarder in the final quarter.

Carlson completely dominated the statistics with 405 yards total offense, 185 on the ground and 220 in the air. The Tigers massed 22 first downs and were penalized 150 yards!

## GAME STATISTICS

|  | Vernon | Carlson |
|---|---|---|
| First downs | 18 | 22 |
| Rushing yardage | 65 | 185 |
| Passing yardage | 60 | 220 |
| Total offense | 125 | 405 |
| Passes att-comp. | 22-4 | 30-18 |
| Passes Intercepted by | 0 | 2 |
| Punts-average | 4-30 | 2-45 |
| Fumbles-no. lost | 3-3 | 1-1 |
| Yards penalized | 95 | 150 |

## SCORE BY QUARTERS

| | | | | |
|---|---|---|---|---|
| Vernon | 8 | 0 | 0 | 6—14 |
| Carlson | 14 | 6 | 20 | 0—44 |

VER—Johnson to Richardson 55 pass
CARL—Narcisse to Mitchell 70 pass
CARL —Narcisse to Mitchell 50 pass
CARL—Narcisse to Mitchell 70 pass
CARL—Narcisse to Mitchell 70 puss
CARL—Jacket 40 interception return
CARL—Francois 25 run
VER—Johnson to Richardson 15 pass

The above four photos were discovered in the 1970 Leesville High School Yearbook, as a tribute to the final football season at Vernon High School

58

VHS HOMECOMING QUEEN--Vernon High School principal, Fletcher Cheatham presents Homecoming Queen, Barbara Williams, with a bouquet during halftime activities of the Vernon Lions-Grand Avenue football game held Saturday in Wampus Cat stadium. The Lions defeated the DeQuincy team by a score of 18 to 6 Other royalty of the court not shown included Vernon Jr. High School Queen Janice Bailey, Vernon Elementary Queen Myrtis Cranson and Football Sweetheart, Leola Fisher (Photo by Earl s Studio)

# The End of the Era

The Lions played their last game in October of 1969.   The final season for the famed team ended with a winning record, as was the tradition of the school and of Foster Thomas' teams.

On November 3, 1969, Vernon High School and Leesville High School were merged into a single school location on Leesville's campus.

Players from Vernon's team would be immediately impactful for the Leesville Wampus Cats.   In 1970, Glover Carter raced for 228 yards in a single game for the Wampus Cats, making him one of the first players in LHS history to eclipse the 200-yard barrier.   Lorenzo Garner would make First Team All-District running back in 1972, making him the first African American football player to earn All-District honors at LHS.

Foster Thomas was hired as an Assistant Coach at Leesville and was on the sidelines for 3 seasons, until he was promoted to the position of Assistant Principal, where he served until 1982.  Coach Thomas deserves undying and ever-lasting credit for his pivotal role in the merger and integration of the two schools in Leesville.   He stepped into a complex breach, and like many at VHS and LHS, reconciled to make the situation work, even though the politics and social environment said otherwise.

The brand and excitement level of football at Leesville changed when the athletes from Vernon came over from Nona Street.   The level of winning at Vernon has never been achieved by any football team in Vernon Parish, but hope remains eternal for a season of state championship glory.  All football in Leesville and Vernon Parish will forever be measured against the greatness of the VHS Lions.   Below is a picture of the first year of football at Leesville with athletes from Vernon suiting up for their new school.   Vernon players are annotated below.

Bottom Row   83--Terry Allen; 24--Alvin Johnson; 26--Joe Gilbert
Third Row   60--Sammy Lee Johnson
Top Row   20--Donnie Gilbert; 23--Glover Carter; 34--Jerry Haynes; 64--JT Buckley; 21--Hilbert Harris

Special Addendum

Much history remains to be written.   Vernon High School's long tradition of educating the African American citizens of Leesville deserves its own, stand-alone history.  It is the hope of this author the project will one day be undertaken and the history of the achievements of VHS will be in one location.   Until such time, this addendum to the history of the VHS Lions will is offered as a tribute to the faculty, staff and students at Vernon is as a placeholder and a challenge for other historians and researchers.

VHS ceased operations in November of 1969 when the students at Vernon's high school and elementary schools were moved to other schools in the Leesville area.   The final class to be graduated from Vernon High School was 1969.   No documentation or list of the faculty nor students from the Fall semester of 1969 could be found.   Further, no yearbook for the 1968-69 yearbook was discovered in research for this effort.  However, the 1965 and 1968 yearbooks were available are the basis for this special addendum.   Faculty and staff members from the 64-65 and 67-68 school years and the students in high school from those school years are provided as a tribute to all of the Lions.   It is hoped that other documentation can be found in research in future years.

# Faculty

MRS. BERTHA HARRISON
First Grade
B. S. Grambling College
M. Ed. Texas Southern
Hobbies - Cooking, Reading, Traveling
V. P. T. A.

MISS IVORY THOMAS
First Grade
L. E. A., P. T. A.

MRS. LILLIAN NABORS
First Grade
B. S. Grambling College
Hobbies - Cooking, Reading
L. E. A., V. P. T. A.

MRS. LYDIA BURSH
Second Grade
B. S. Grambling College
Hobbies - Dancing, Reading,
Singing, Sports
L. E. A., Modern Dance
Group, Majorettes

MRS. FLOSSIE TRAYLOR
Second Grade
B. S. Grambling College
Hobbies - Sewing, Reading, Fishing
L. E. A., V. P. T. A.

MRS. RENA THOMAS
Second Grade
Hobbies - Bowling, Horse-
back Riding
L. E. A., V. P. T. A.

MRS. RUBY DELTON
Social Studies
B. S. Grambling College
Piano Playing and Reading the Bible
L. E. A.

MR. GORDIE HOLT
English and Speech
B. S. Grambling College
Hobbies - Bowling, Dancing,
Reading
Co-Sponsor Nat'l Honor Society,
Debating Team

MRS. MAXINE GUNN
Math and Social Studies
B. S. Southern University
Hobbies - Reading, Movies, Television
N. M. T. A., V. P. T. A.,
Debating Team

MRS. ORGERINE SMITH
Physical Ed. and Reading
B. S. Grambling College
Hobbies - Sewing,
Television, Sports
Girls Basketball Coach

MRS. KATHERINE CARROLL
Special Education
B. S. Jacksonville University
Hobbies - Handicraft, Sewing,
Home Decorating
L. T. A., N. E. A.

MR. EDWARD BEAUCHAMP
Foreign Lang., English
B. A. Dillard University
Hobby - Reading
V. P. T. A.

MRS. MYRTHA DIXON JOHNSON
English, Librarian
B. S. Grambling
Hobbies - Reading, Experimenting
with Food
V. P. T. A.

MR. SAMUEL BURSH
Coach, Math
B. S. Grambling
Hobbies - Sports,
Singing
L. E. A., N. C. T. M.,
V. P. T. A.

MRS. MARTHA R. WHITE
Home Economics
B. S. Grambling
Hobbies - Collecting photos and
recipes, Cooking, and Sewing

MR. BOBBY CONERLY
Commerce and Civics
B. S. Southern Univ.
Hobbies - Sports and
Music
L. E. A., L. V. A.,
V. P. T. A., L. B. A.

MRS. JANET HOLLAND
Art
B. F. A. Drake Univ.
Hobbies - Sewing, Swimming, Painting
L. T. A., N. E. A., N. A. E. A.

MR. JAMES SOWELLS
Industrial Arts
B. S. Grambling
Hobbies - Reading
and Drawing
V. P. T. A.

65

MRS. ALICE GRAF
Reading Specialist
B. A. Univ. of Mass.
M. A. Boston Univ.
Hobbies - Reading, Sewing,
Home Decorating, Sports
L. T. A.

MR. LEONARD DAVIS
Band Director
B. S. Southern Univ.
Hobby - Model
Airplanes
V. P. T. A.

MR. FOSTER THOMAS
Head Coach, Phsycial Ed.,
Driver Education
B. S. Grambling College
Hobbies - Sports, Reading
P. E. L. State, V. P. T. A.

MR. GENE DAVIS
Chorus Director
B. S. Grambling
Hobbies - Model
Airplanes, Painting
L. E. A., V. P. T. A.

MRS. ALMA BROWN
Gen. Science and Biology
B. S. Wiley College
M. Ed. Texas Southern Univ.
Hobbies - Reading, Traveling,
Collecting unusual Ash trays and
Cooking
L. E. A., N. S. T. A., V. P. T. A.,
Future Scientists of America

MRS. DOROTHY PERKINS
Guidance Counselor
B. S. Southern Univ.
M. A. Texas Southern
Univ.
Hobbies - Bowling,
Listening to Music
V. P. G. A., L. E. A.,
V. P. T. A.
Adult Educ. Teacher
Co-Sponsor: National
Honor Society

MR. HAMP SMITH
Principal, Vernon Elementary
B.S. Grambling College
Hobbies - Reading and Sports
L.E.A., E.P.A., V.P.T.A.

MR. FLETCHER CHEATHAM
Principal, Vernon
High School
B.S. Grambling
M.Ed. Univ. of
Southwestern La.
Hobbies - Reading,
Traveling, Sports,
Discussing Inter-
national Politics
L.E.A., V.P.T.A.,
N.A.S.S.P.

# Teachers' Aids

MISS MARGARET MONTGOMERY

MRS. LOYCE FISHER

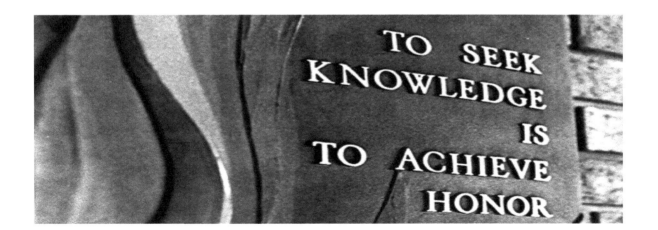

TO SEEK
KNOWLEDGE
IS
TO ACHIEVE
HONOR

# Lunchroom Employees

Mrs. J. Wesley, Mrs. O. Williams, Mrs. A. Thomas, Mrs. W. Jones, Mrs. H. Rock, Mrs. R. Penn, Mrs. E. Laborde, Mrs. M. Moore.

# Custodians

Mr. R. Edison, Mrs. M. Allen, Mr. K. Williams, Mr. L. Patterson.

# Bus Drivers

Mr. J. Sowells, Mr. O. Brown, Mr. E. Page, Mr. L. Joiner.

Vernon High School Class of 1968
2<sup>nd</sup> to last Class at VHS

COLVIN, SUSIE
Choir

CONERLY, BETTY ANN

CROWELL, GWENDOLYN
Choir, Band, National Honor
Society, Debating Team

FOSTER, MARVIN
Chaplain, Football, Track,
Choir

GARNER, BRENDA
Assistant Secretary, Modern
Dance, Miss Vernon High 1967-
68, Band, Debating Team,
Choir

JONES, ADA
Choir, Band

JONES, HENRY

KEYS, BEATRICE
Choir, Secretary

LEWIS, ANNETTE
Choir

MARSH, KATHRYN
Miss Senior 1967-68, Treas-
urer, Basketball, Choir

MOORE, JOHN HENRY
Choir

Vernon High School Juniors in 1968
Vernon High School Seniors in 1969 – Last Class at VHS

Blow, Betty
Brown, Lois
Bursh, Leandrea

Cooper, Gregory
Ellis, Arthur
Fisher, John

Ford, Hattie
Gay, Charles
Haynes, Patsy

Hopkins, Louis
Johnson, Dorothy
King, Dorothy

Mallet, Michael
Martin, Thomas
Mattox, Venita

Robinson, Donna
Robinson, Martha
Sawyer, Earnest

Slater, Marie
Smith, Alice
Smith, Clyde

Smith, Louis
Spearman, Rose
Warren, Carolyn

Wesley, Hilton
Wilson, Calvin
Wilson, Cassandra

Wilson, Dorothy
Wood, Cecil

# Vernon High School Sophomores in 1968
## (Seniors in 1970 at Leesville)

Blow, Robert
Brown, Teresa
Brown, Jerry
Clark, Jewel

Coine, Jerry
Cooper, Cornell
Drain, Lorraine
Fisher, Leola

Grant, Isaac
Greening, Ruby
Hicks, Murray
Jackson, Faye

Johnson, Leonard
Jones, Hosie
Keys, Etter
Madria, Leon

Marsh, Hazel
Moore, Jimmie
Morris, Glenda
Pratt, Carolyn

Pratt, Linda
Price, Travis
Rock, Donald
Smith, Thelma

Sowells, Henry
Strahan, Essie
Tinsley, Mose
Taylor, Lynda

Warren, Elois
Williams, Barbara
Wells, Regina
Wilson, Ervin

Wilson, Jerry
Haynes, Antione
Jones, Michael

## Vernon High School Freshmen in 1968
## (Seniors at Leesville in 1971)

Acey, Ledale
Allen, Douglas
Barrow, Clinton
Brown, Cathy
Brown, Douglas

Brown, Joyce
Brown, Linda
Brown, Wanda
Carter, Glover
Chipp, Betty

Conerly, Bernell
Drain, Joe
Dudley, William
Ellis, Janice
Ford, Betty

Ford, Lawrence
Garner, Willie
Gilbert, Donnie
Grant, Edna
Great, Lenora

Green, Jacqueline
Harris, Josephine
Hawkins, Mildred
Haynes, Jerry
Haynes, Jimmie

Hickman, JoVeder
Hill, Alma
Holmes, Rosetta
Hudson, James
Jackson, Henry

Johnson, Clinton
Joiner, Emma

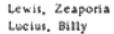

Lewis, Zeaporia
Lucius, Billy

Magee, Patricia
Martin, Johnny
Martin, Lawrence
McIntosh, Bobby
Reggans, Sarah

Richard, Earl
Robinson, Clara
Rushing, Janie
Scott, Ralph
Sheppard, Olando

Sibley, Willie
Smith, Lillie
Smith, Shirley
Sowells, Patricia
Sowells, Roosevelt

Staton, Lottie
Thomas, Sherry
Upshaw, Carolyn
Upshaw, Linda
Walker, Joyce

Wallace, Sonny
Warren, Barbara
Warren, Jesse
Webb, Henry
Wesley, Milton

Williams, Glenda
Williams, Loretta
Wilson, Chauncey
Wilson, Kenneth
Woods, Deliah

75

# VHS Faculty 1964-65 School Year

MRS. LILLIAN NABORS
First Grade
B. S. Grambling College
Hobbies - Reading and Cooking

MRS. BERTHA HARRISON
First Grade
B. S. Grambling College
M. Ed. Texas Southern
University
Hobbies - Cooking, Reading
and Traveling

MRS. NELLIE FRANCIS
First Grade
Grambling College
Hobbies - Singing, Reading and
Piano Playing

MRS. FLOSSIE TRAYLOR
Second Grade
B. S. Grambling College
Hobbies - Sewing and Reading

MRS. LYDIA BURSH
Second Grade
B. S. Grambling College
Hobbies - Modern Dancing,
Singing, and Reading

MRS. VERONE CHAPPELL
Second Grade
B. S. Grambling College
Hobbies - Sewing, Dancing and
Playing Games

MRS. WILLIE MAE SINGLETON
Third Grade
B. S. Grambling College
Hobby - Reading

MISS BARBARA BARROW
Third Grade
B. A. Southern University
Hobbies - Crocheting, Reading
and Traveling

MRS. MARY CHEATHAM
Third Grade
B. S. Grambling College
Hobbies - Reading, Dancing and
Designing Clothes

MRS. GLADYS McLAURIN
Fourth Grade
B. S. Southern University
Hobbies - Reading and Cooking

MRS. PATRICIA THOMAS
Fourth Grade
B. S. Grambling College
Hobbies - Fishing, Sewing and
Reading

MRS. JUANITA JOHNSON
Fourth Grade
Grambling College
Hobbies - Swimming, Dancing,
and Cooking

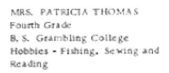

MRS. CORA WILSON
Fifth Grade
B. S. Grambling College
Hobbies - Music, Television
and Reading

MRS. MILDRED SELF
Fifth Grade
B. S. Grambling College
Hobbies - Reading, Social
work and Cooking

MRS. ROSA NELL BATTISTE
Sixth Grade
B. S. Grambling College
M. Ed. Texas Southern
University
Hobbies - Collecting
Handkerchiefs and Reading

MR. HAMP SMITH
Sixth Grade
B. S. Grambling College
Hobbies - Fishing, Hunting
and Reading

MR. SAMUEL BURSH
Jr. High Math and Algebra I
B. S. Grambling College
Hobbies - Sports and Music

MR. FLETCHER CHEATHAM
Jr. High Science and Reading
B. S. Grambling College
Hobbies - Reading, Golf and
Talking

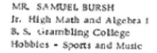

MRS. MARY HICKERSON
English
B. S. Grambling College
Hobbies - Reading and Piano
Playing

MR. FOSTER THOMAS
Jr. High Social Studies
and P. E.
B. S. Grambling College
Hobby - Golf

MRS. ALMA BROWN
General Science, Biology and
Chemistry
B. S. Wiley College
M. Ed. Texas Southern
University
Hobbies - Reading, Cooking,
Bowling and Traveling
Science Honor Club

MRS. JOYCE PRESTON
English and Spanish
B. A. Southern University
Hobbies - Reading, Sewing and
Crossword Puzzles

MRS. MYRTHA DIXON JOHNSON
English - Library
B. S. Grambling College
Hobbies - Cooking and Reading
F. T. A. and Library Clubs

MRS. RUBY HIGGINS
Home Economics
B. S. Grambling College
Hobbies - Cooking, Sewing,
and Horseback Riding
N. H. A. and Home Economics
Clubs

MRS. MAXINE GUNN
Algebra I, Plane Geometry,
Senior Math., and American
History
B. S. Southern University
Hobbies - Reading and Movies
Mathematicians of
Tomorrow Club
National Honor Society

MISS VELMA WAGNER
Special Education
B. S. Grambling College
Hobbies - Reading, Riding,
and Driving

A group of teachers
chat after the
Christmas Cantata

MRS. DOROTHY PERKINS
School Counselor
B. S. Southern University
M. A. Texas Southern
University
Hobbies - Reading, Bowling and
Swimming
Adult Education Teacher
National Honor Society

MR. BOBBY CONERLY
Commerce
B. S. Southern University
Hobbies - Listening to Music and
Reading

MR. JOSEPH DEAMER
Industrial Arts and General
Math.
B. S. Southern University
Hobby - Sports

MRS. ORGERINE SMITH
Reading and Physical
Education
B. S. Grambling College
Hobby - Sewing
Basketball Coach

MR. LEONARD DAVIS
Music and Jr. High Social
Studies
B. S. Southern University
Hobbies - Airplane Modeling
Dance Music
Band Director

MR. GENE HARREL DAVIS
Choral Music
B. A. Grambling College
Hobbies - Reading and Singing
Choir Director

Mrs. Dixon, Brown, Gunn,
and Mr. Cheatham discuss
a mutual problem with
Counselor, Perkins.

81

## Custodians

Mamie Allen, Roosevelt Edison, Kenneth Williams, Lim Patterson.

## Bus Drivers

Harold Wright, Raymond Joiner, Omner Brown, Victor Harvey, Jesse Sowells

## Lunchroom Staff

Lola Johnson
Grace Spearman
Rosie Penn
Standing:
Jessie Wesley,
    Lunchroom Super-
    visor

Evelyn Randle
Sarah Powell
Mary Moore
Not pictured:
Ola Drumgoole
Classie Cage

Vernon High School Class of 1965

## Seniors

BELL, BRENDA

BLACK, ROBERT
  Band, Football

BRITTON, MAMIE
  Basketball
  Choir

DICKERSON, ROBERT
  President Math
  Club, Football

GAINES, DAVID
  Football

JOHNSON, JESSE
  Band

KENNEDY, CLARENCE
  Vice Pres. Math
  Club, Basketball
  Football
  National Honor
        Society

LEWIS, BETTY
  Choir, Math
  Club

McDUFFEY, LULA
  Choir

83

MORISE, BILLY
Math Club,
Basketball,
Band, Football

PENN, HOUSTON
Band, Choir

POLAND, DONALD
Band, Choir,
Basketball Trainer

SAWYER, QUINCY
Choir, Band

SIMPSON, VIRGINIA
Majorette

WILLIAMS, AZA

WILLIAMS, FRANKIE
Vice Pres. Senior
Class, Football

WILLIAMS, RICHARD
Pres. Senior Class,
Football, Band,
Basketball

WILLIAMS, STEVE
Football

84

# Vernon High School Juniors in 1965
## (Class of 1966)

Allen, Emma
Blow, Katherine
Britton, Mary
Brown, Charlotte

Brown, Irma
Brown, Mary
Brown, Ormer
Burnett, James

Cooper, Christopher
Cooper, Marcus
Crowell, Willie
Drain, Donald

Garner, Glen
Gilbert, Shirley
Guiton, Barbara
Hicks, Peggy

Johnson, Andrew
Johnson, Janice
Judkins, Auther

Martin, Eddie
Montgomery, Margaret
Phillips, Carolyn
Quiney, Shirley

Robinson, Robert
Sibley, Fred
Sibley, Murkel
Sibley, Retha

Smith, Johnny
Sowell, Maxie
Spearman, Mary
Spencer, Alfred

Wells, Gloria
Wesley, Evelyn
Williams, Beverly
Williams, Clinton

Wilson, Corneola
Wilson, Jacqueline
Wood, Orland

# Vernon High School Sophomores in 1965)
## (Class of 1967)

Barrow, Charles
Burns, Vera
Burton, Obie
Cage, Alcina
Clarkston, Joe

Cooper, Ronald
Crowell, Phillip
Daniels, James
Davis, John
Davis, Norma

Davis, Ocie
Dotson, Melvin
Ellis, Thomas
Fleming, R.
Foster, John

Garner, Wade
Hawkins, Joanna
Hickmon, Emma
Howard, Carl

Jackson, LeRoy
Johnson, Ella
Johnson, Leevester

Keys, Leese
Mallet, Donald
Mattox, Theresa
Moore, George
Morris, Regina

Morris, Sheryl
Nason, Dot
Prince, Carolyn
Queen, John
Robinson, R.

Rowe, Barbara
Smith, Charles
Smith, J. T.
Smith, Sue
Spearman, Ruby

Steiner, David
Turner, Lucy
Warren, Donnie
Warren, Harold

Wilson, Alvoy
Wilson, Sheppard
Wood, Milton

# Vernon High School Freshmen in 1968
## (Class of 1965)

Chiley, Bernice
Colvin, Susie
Conerly, Betty
Crowell, Gwendolyn

Deans, Margaret
Dunlap, Earnest
Edwards, Eddie
Foster, Marvin

Gamer, Brenda
Gill, Nellie
Grant, Sandra
Green, Henry

Johnson, Brenda
Johnson, Clarence
Johnson, Dorothy
Jones, Ada Lee

Keys, Beatrice
King, Dorothy
Lee, Ralph

Absent
PHOTO
NOT AVAILABLE

Moore, John
Payton, Vernon
Pea, Archie
Puckett, Melvin

Quiney, Shelton
Richard, Charles
Richard, Timothy
Robinson, Levander

Robinson, Martha
Sanders, Patricia
Smith, Bertha
Smith, Billie Sue

Sowell, Frank
Sowells, Lionel
Strahan, Johnnie
Suel, Sammie

Tatum, Jesse
Williams, Barbara
Wilson, Mattie
Wood, Huey

## Special Thanks

This book could not have been created nor produced without the assistance of a number of people   VHS alumni JT Smith was my primary research teammate in this endeavor.   JT arranged a very special luncheon with former Lion players and school leaders to help me craft and then finalize the document.   Mrs. Maxine Gunn, Mr. Fletcher Cheatham and Mr. Sam Bursh deserve special recognition for their contributions to the effort.   Sam created the cover on the book and Mr. Cheatham and Mrs. Gunn provided important information to me as I pieced this effort together. I hope this history project meets their high standards.

I must pay a special, never-ending tribute to Coach Foster Thomas.   Coach Thomas was an Assistant Principal at Leesville during my high school years and I always knew him as a strong leader and man of integrity.  He was integral in our community and he helped make Leesville High a great school.  I revered him for my entire life.   The legend of the Lions has always been alive and well in Leesville, but I have seen little on it for most of my life.   The accomplishment of Vernon was more legend than documented fact to me.  I wanted to see things written down.

My wife, Carolyn and my daughter Emma went with me to Fort Worth to interview Coach in 2013 to try and begin this project.   We spent a wonderful day with Foster, his beautiful wife Pat (who taught me Louisiana History), Mr. Gordie Holt (who taught me Junior English) and Terry Holt (my LHS teammate) and heard many of these stories firsthand, for the first time.   The conversation stoked in my spirit a desire to piece this book together.   My heart has ached to craft as much of this tale as possible, and rest assured I am not finished writing about VHS and the school's impact on Leesville.

For now, the I offer up this book as a tribute to the Mighty Vernon Lions.

Seated:  Foster Thomas.   Standing L-R Charles Owen, Terry Holt, Gordie Holt

# Index

| | | | | | | |
|---|---|---|---|---|---|---|
| Abram | | 33 | Bursh | Lee | 31 |
| Allen | Mamie | 82 | Bursh | Lydia | 76 |
| Allen | Mrs. M. | 68 | Bursh | Sam | 91 |
| Allen | Terry | 61 | Bursh | Samuel | 28 |
| Bailey | Janice | 60 | Bursh | Samuel | 47 |
| Barrow | Barbara | 77 | Bursh | Samuel | 49 |
| Barrow | C. | 53 | Bursh | Samuel | 65 |
| Batiste | Rosa Nell | 78 | Bursh | Samuel | 78 |
| Beauchamp | Edward | 64 | Cage | Claude | 82 |
| Beltfessol | Mack | 32 | Calvin | Jimmie | 47 |
| Bennett | Delma | 12 | Carroll | Katherine | 64 |
| Black | Robert | 25 | Carter | Glover | 53 |
| Blue | Vida | 34 | Carter | Glover | 61 |
| Blue | Vida | 35 | Carter | Jerry | 37 |
| Booke | Professor | 3 | Cate | Ross | 38 |
| Brown | Alma | 66 | Chappell | Verone | 76 |
| Brown | Alma | 79 | Cheatam | Fletcher | 3 |
| Brown | Jerry | 47 | Cheatam | | 4 |
| Brown | Leonard | 7 | Cheatham | Fletcher | 28 |
| Brown | Mr. O | 68 | Cheatham | Fletcher | 47 |
| Brown | Omner | 82 | Cheatham | Fletcher | 51 |
| Brown | Richard | 11 | Cheatham | Fletcher | 53 |
| Bucklet | JT | 53 | Cheatham | Fletcher | 60 |
| Buckley | John | 52 | Cheatham | Fletcher | 67 |
| Buckley | JT | 35 | Cheatham | Fletcher | 78 |
| Buckley | JT | | Cheatham | Fletcher | 91 |
| Buckley | JT | 61 | Cheatham | Mary | 77 |
| Burkehead | Tyron | 15 | Clarkson | Joe | 25 |
| Burns | Herbert | 16 | Clarkson | Joseph | 16 |
| Burns | Herbert | 17 | Close | Amous | 55 |
| Burns | Herbert | 20 | Coin | Jerry | 47 |
| Burns | Herbert | 22 | Collins | Clarence | 55 |
| Burns | Herbert | 24 | conerly | Bobby | 65 |
| Burns | Herbert | 25 | Conerly | Bobby | 80 |
| Burns | Herbert | 26 | Cranson | Myrtis | 60 |
| Burns | Herbert | 29 | Davis | Freddie | 47 |
| Burns | Herbert | 31 | Davis | Gene | 81 |
| Burns | Robert | 14 | Davis | Leonard | 66 |
| Burns | Robert | 23 | Davis | Leonard | 81 |
| Bursch | Samuel | 35 | Davis | | 33 |
| Bursh | Leandrea | 35 | Davis | Gene | 66 |

| | | | | | |
|---|---|---|---|---|---|
| Deamer | Joseph | 4 | Foster | Marvin | 46 |
| Deamer | Joseph | 5 | Foster | Marvin | 47 |
| Deamer | Joseph | 28 | Francis | Nellie | 76 |
| Deamer | Joseph | 49 | Gaines | David | 14 |
| Deamer | Joseph | 81 | Gaines | David | 22 |
| Dejean | Paul | 12 | Gaines | David | 23 |
| Delton | Ruby | 64 | Gaines | David | 24 |
| Dickerson | Robert | 8 | Gaines | David | 26 |
| Dickerson | Robert | 14 | Gaines | David | 26 |
| Dickerson | Robert | 15 | Garber | Wade | 35 |
| Dickerson | Robert | 16 | Garner | Glen | 22 |
| Dickerson | Robert | 17 | Garner | Glen | 31 |
| Dickerson | Robert | 18 | Garner | Lorenzo | 61 |
| Dickerson | Robert | 20 | Garner | Richard | 25 |
| Dossman | Curley | 13 | Garner | Willie | 47 |
| Dotson | Melvin | 35 | Garrett | Jack | 8 |
| Douglas | Jewel | 13 | Gatson | | 33 |
| Drain | Joe | 47 | Gilbert | Donnie | 39 |
| Drain | Joe Lee | 35 | Gilbert | Donnie | 45 |
| Drake | Charles | 32 | Gilbert | Donnie | 49 |
| Drake | Charles | 38 | Gilbert | Donnie | 52 |
| Drumgoole | Ola | 82 | Gilbert | Donnie | 53 |
| Edison | Mr. R. | 68 | Gilbert | Donnie | 61 |
| Edison | Roosevelt | 82 | Gilbert | Joe | 61 |
| Edwards | Harold | 55 | Goodwin | Lionel | 7 |
| Elliott | Errol | 55 | Goodwin | Willard | 9 |
| Ellis | Arthur | 35 | Graf | Alice | 66 |
| Ellis | Thomas | 35 | Grant | I.T. | 46 |
| Farris | Alvin | 11 | Grant | Isaac | 47 |
| Fischer | Murphy | 35 | Grant | L.T. | 52 |
| Fisher | James | 47 | Gray | Cecil | 41 |
| Fisher | Leola | 60 | Gray | Freddie | 11 |
| Fisher | Loyce | 67 | Green | Howad | 38 |
| Fisher | Murphy | 49 | Guillory | Buddis | 12 |
| Floyd | Richard | 55 | Gunn | Maxine | 64 |
| Fontenot | Hayward | 54 | Gunn | Maxine | 80 |
| Ford | Gu | 33 | Gunn | Maxine | 91 |
| Ford | John | 33 | Harris | Charles | 9 |
| Foreman | Percy | 33 | Harris | Hilbert | 61 |
| Foster | John | 25 | Harrison | Bertha | 76 |
| Foster | Marvin | 34 | Harrison | Bethea | 63 |
| Foster | Marvin | 35 | Harvey | Victor | 82 |
| Foster | Marvin | 36 | Haynes | Albert | 35 |
| Foster | Marvin | 39 | Haynes | Anton | 31 |
| Foster | Marvin | 42 | Haynes | Antonny | 35 |

| | | | | | |
|---|---|---|---|---|---|
| Haynes | Jerry | 47 | Jackson | Henry | 43 |
| Haynes | Jerry | 52 | Jackson | Henry | 47 |
| Haynes | Jerry | 53 | Jackson | Henry | 52 |
| Haynes | Jerry | 61 | Jackson | LeRoy | 35 |
| Haynes | Jimmy | 47 | Jackson | Leroy | 52 |
| Haynes | | 4 | Jefferson | Louis | 8 |
| Hetarie | Earl | 36 | Jefferson | Louis | 14 |
| Hickerson | Mary | 79 | Jefferson | Louis | 15 |
| Higgins | Ruby | 79 | Jefferson | Louis | 17 |
| Holand | Janet | 65 | Jefferson | Louis | 18 |
| Holt | Gordie | 64 | Jefferson | Louis | 19 |
| Holt | Gordie | 91 | Jefferson | | 4 |
| Holt | Terry | 91 | Johnsoin | Louis | 51 |
| Hopkins | Louis | 39 | Johnson | Allen | 56 |
| Hopkins | Louis | 40 | Johnson | Alvin | 61 |
| Hopkins | Louis | 47 | Johnson | Andrew | 15 |
| Hopkins | Louis | 51 | Johnson | G | 53 |
| Hopkins | Louis | 52 | Johnson | Gary | 47 |
| Howard | Carl | 10 | Johnson | Juanita | 77 |
| Howard | Carl | 12 | Johnson | Lemon | 34 |
| Howard | Carl | 14 | Johnson | Lemon | 38 |
| Howard | Carl | 15 | Johnson | Leon | 36 |
| Howard | Carl | 17 | Johnson | Leonard | 35 |
| Howard | Carl | 18 | Johnson | Leonard | 37 |
| Howard | Carl | 19 | Johnson | Leonard | 39 |
| Howard | Carl | 20 | Johnson | Leonard | 40 |
| Howard | Carl | 22 | Johnson | Leonard | 41 |
| Howard | Carl | 23 | Johnson | Leonard | 42 |
| Howard | Carl | 24 | Johnson | Leonard | 47 |
| Howard | Carl | 25 | Johnson | Leonard | 51 |
| Howard | Carl | 26 | Johnson | Leonard | 52 |
| Howard | Carl | 27 | Johnson | Lois | 82 |
| Howard | Carl | 28 | Johnson | Myrtha | 65 |
| Howard | Carl | 29 | Johnson | Myrtha | 79 |
| Howard | Carl | 30 | Johnson | Robert | 15 |
| Howard | Carl | 31 | Johnson | Sam | 53 |
| Howard | Carl | 31 | Johnson | Sammy Lee | 61 |
| Howard | Carl | 32 | Joiner | Mr. L. | 68 |
| Howard | Carl | 33 | Joiner | Raymond | 82 |
| Jacket | Todd | 56 | Jones | Hosie | 47 |
| Jackson | Elmo | 35 | Jones | Lloyd | 36 |
| Jackson | Henry | 25 | Jones | Michael | 52 |
| Jackson | Henry | 31 | Jones | Michael | 53 |
| Jackson | Henry | 35 | Jones | Mrs. W. | 68 |
| Jackson | Henry | 42 | Kelly | Geoerge | 7 |

| | | | | | | |
|---|---|---|---|---|---|---|
| Kelly | Joseph | 7 | Martin | Thomas | 50 |
| Kennedy | Clarence | 22 | McCoy | Nathaniel | 54 |
| Kennedy | Clarence | 25 | McCoy | Nathaniel | 55 |
| Kennedy | Steve | 8 | McGee | Willie | 37 |
| Kennedy | Clarence | 23 | McKeever | Edward | 27 |
| Laborde | Mrs. E. | 68 | McLaurin | Gladys | 77 |
| Lafleur | Inez | 13 | McMahon | Bluitt | 36 |
| Lavergne | Linus | 55 | McMahon | Ralph | 36 |
| Lee | Ralph | 24 | McNeal | Gerald | 41 |
| Lee | Ralph | 31 | Miller | | 4 |
| Lee | Ralph | 34 | Mitchell | Johnny | 56 |
| Lee | Ralph | 35 | Monroe | Robert | 37 |
| Lee | Ralph | 36 | Montgomery | Margaret | 67 |
| Lee | Richard | 12 | Moore | Mary | 82 |
| Lewis | Calvin | 46 | Moore | Mrs. M. | 68 |
| Lincoln | Major | 17 | Mouton | Leroy | 13 |
| Madria | Leon | 30 | Nabors | Lillian | 63 |
| Madria | Leon | 31 | Nabors | Lillian | 76 |
| Madria | Leon | 35 | Narcisse | Larry | 56 |
| Madria | Leon | 37 | Page | Mr. E | 68 |
| Madria | Leon | 39 | Patterson | Lim | 82 |
| Madria | Leon | 41 | Patterson | Mr. L. 68 | 68 |
| Madria | Leon | 42 | Pea | Archie | 24 |
| Madria | Leon | 43 | Penn | Mrs. R. | 68 |
| Madria | Leon | 47 | Penn | Rose | 82 |
| Madria | Leonard | 29 | Perkins | Dorothy | 66 |
| Mallet | Don | 34 | Perkins | Dorothy | 80 |
| Mallet | Don | 36 | Perkins | James | 4 |
| Mallet | Donald | 35 | Peters | John | 32 |
| Mallet | Michael | 31 | Pinkney | Randolph | 37 |
| Mallet | Michael | 34 | Porter | | 7 |
| Mallet | Michael | 35 | Powell | Sarah | 82 |
| Mallet | Michael | 39 | Preston | Joyce | 79 |
| Mallet | Michael | 40 | Puckett | Melvin | 31 |
| Mallet | Michael | 42 | Pullman | Seymour | 7 |
| Mallet | Michael | 43 | Quiney | Shelton | 35 |
| Mallet | Michael | 44 | Randle | Evelyn | 82 |
| Mallet | Michael | 47 | Reado | John | 32 |
| Mallet | Michael | 51 | Redfud | William | 12 |
| Mallet | Michael | 52 | Richard | Charles | 47 |
| Mallet | Mike | 36 | Richard | Julius | 47 |
| Martin | James | 4 | Richards | Charles | 35 |
| Martin | Johnny | 47 | Richardson | Warren | 56 |
| Martin | Johnny | 52 | Rigmalden | Thomas | 7 |
| Martin | Thomas | 47 | Robinson | Roy | 23 |

| | | | | | | |
|---|---|---|---|---|---|---|
| Robinson | Roy | 24 | | Smith | JT | 29 |
| Robinson | Roy | 26 | | Smith | JT | 30 |
| Robinson | Roy | 31 | | Smith | JT | 31 |
| Robinson | Roy | 35 | | Smith | JT | 32 |
| Robinson | Roy | 37 | | Smith | JT | 34 |
| Robinson | Tommie Joe | 16 | | Smith | JT | 35 |
| Robinson | Tommie Joe | 18 | | Smith | JT | 37 |
| Rock | Donald | 35 | | Smith | JT | 38 |
| Rock | Mrs. H. | 68 | | Smith | JT | 91 |
| Romar | Michael | 55 | | Smith | Lewis | 35 |
| Ross | Charles | 38 | | Smith | Lewis | 40 |
| Rowe | Thadeus | 35 | | Smith | Louis | 41 |
| Rushen | Roy | 3 | | Smith | Louis | 46 |
| Rushen | Roy | 17 | | Smith | Louis | 47 |
| Rushen | Roy | 21 | | Smith | Orgerine | 64 |
| Sawyer | Earnest | 42 | | Smith | Orgerine | 81 |
| Sawyer | Earnest | 50 | | Snow | Curtis | 51 |
| Sawyer | Ernest | 35 | | Sowell | Mr. J. | 68 |
| Scott | John | 54 | | Sowells | Jesse | 82 |
| Scott | Ralph | 47 | | Sowels | James | 65 |
| Self | Mildred | 78 | | Spearman | Grace | 82 |
| Shankle | Leeman | 9 | | Spencer | Alfred | 24 |
| Shankle | Leemon | 12 | | Spencer | Alfred | 31 |
| Shankle | Leemon | 27 | | Spencer | Alfred | 33 |
| Shankle | Leon | 32 | | Spencer | | 30 |
| Sibley | Muncie | 30 | | Spiller | James | 11 |
| Simms | Robert | 24 | | Stephens | James High | |
| Sims | | 33 | | | School | 13 |
| Singleton | Willie Mae | 77 | | Stevenson | Elisjah | 37 |
| Skinner | Claiborne | 37 | | Taylor | Joe | 31 |
| Smith | Charles | 16 | | Thierry | Clarence | 55 |
| Smith | Charles | 19 | | Thierry | Michael | 55 |
| Smith | Charles | 24 | | Thomas | Bobby | 47 |
| Smith | Charles | 25 | | Thomas | Foster | 4 |
| Smith | Hamp | 67 | | Thomas | Foster | 5 |
| Smith | JT | 14 | | Thomas | Foster | 14 |
| Smith | JT | 15 | | Thomas | Foster | 22 |
| Smith | JT | 17 | | Thomas | Foster | 27 |
| Smith | JT | 21 | | Thomas | Foster | 28 |
| Smith | JT | 23 | | Thomas | Foster | 35 |
| Smith | JT | 24 | | Thomas | Foster | 40 |
| Smith | JT | 25 | | Thomas | Foster | 42 |
| Smith | JT | 26 | | Thomas | Foster | 46 |
| Smith | JT | 26 | | Thomas | Foster | 47 |
| Smith | JT | 28 | | Thomas | Foster | 49 |

| | | | | | | |
|---|---|---|---|---|---|---|
| Thomas | Foster | 51 | | Washington | A.K. | 9 |
| Thomas | Foster | 52 | | Washington | A.K. | 12 |
| Thomas | Foster | 53 | | Washington | C.H. | 3 |
| Thomas | Foster | 61 | | Wesley | Hilton | 31 |
| Thomas | Foster | 66 | | Wesley | Hilton | 35 |
| Thomas | Foster | 79 | | Wesley | Hilton | 42 |
| Thomas | Foster | 91 | | Wesley | Hilton | 43 |
| Thomas | Ivory | 63 | | Wesley | Hilton | 47 |
| Thomas | John | 24 | | Wesley | Jessie | 82 |
| Thomas | Mrs. A | 68 | | Wesley | Milton | 35 |
| Thomas | Patricia | 77 | | Wesley | Mrs. J. | 68 |
| Thomas | Rena | 63 | | White | Martha | 65 |
| Thomas | Sherry | 35 | | Wiergate | High | 14 |
| Thomas | Sherry | 47 | | Wiergate | | 4 |
| Tinsley | Mose | 35 | | Williams | Barbara | 60 |
| Tinsley | Mose | 47 | | Williams | Clinton | 15 |
| Tinsley | Mose | 50 | | Williams | Frank | 7 |
| Tinsley | Mose | 53 | | Williams | Frankie | 16 |
| Tinsley | Sylvester | 25 | | Williams | Frankie | 18 |
| Tinsley | Sylvester | 31 | | Williams | Frankie | 22 |
| Traylor | Flossie | 63 | | Williams | Frankie | 24 |
| Traylor | Flossie | 76 | | Williams | Frankie | 26 |
| VHS Class of 1965 | | 83 | | Williams | Frankie | 28 |
| VHS Class of 1966 (as juniors) | | 85 | | Williams | George | 15 |
| VHS Class of 1967 (as sophomores) | | 87 | | Williams | James | 24 |
| VHS Class of 1968 | | 69 | | Williams | Keneth | 82 |
| VHS Class of 1968 (as freshmen) | | 89 | | Williams | LaSalle | 7 |
| VHS Class of 1969 (as juniors) | | 70 | | Williams | LaSalle | 12 |
| | | | | Williams | Lasalle | 32 |
| VHS Freshmen 1968 (LHS Class of 1971) | | 74 | | Williams | Mr. K. | 68 |
| | | | | Williams | Mrs. O | 68 |
| | | | | Williams | Otis | 14 |
| VHS Sophomores 1968 (LHS Class of 1970) | | 72 | | Williams | Stee | 25 |
| | | | | Williams | Steve | 15 |
| Vidrine | Lee | 13 | | Williams | Steve | 20 |
| Wagner | Velma | 80 | | Williams | Steve | 22 |
| Walker | George | 12 | | Williams | Steve | 24 |
| Walker | Irvin | 26 | | Wilson | Alvoy | 25 |
| Wallace | Sonny | 35 | | Wilson | Alvoy | 31 |
| Wallace | Sonny | 47 | | Wilson | Barney | 15 |
| Wallace | Sonny | 52 | | Wilson | Calvin | 35 |
| | | | | Wilson | Calvin | 36 |
| | | | | Wilson | Calvin | 39 |
| | | | | Wilson | Calvin | 45 |
| | | | | Wilson | Calvin | 46 |

| Wilson | Calvin | 47 | Woods | Cecil | 42 |
| Wilson | Calvin | 52 | Woods | Don | 47 |
| Wilson | Cora | 78 | Wright | Harold | 82 |
| Woodard | Gerald | 12 | | | |

CPSIA information can be obtained
at www.ICGtesting.com
Printed in the USA
LVHW020731150323
741653LV00004B/207